NĀ PUA ALIʻI O KAUAʻI

NĀ PUA

ALI'I O KAUA'I

Ruling Chiefs of Kaua'i

Frederick B. Wichman

A LATITUDE 20 BOOK

University of Hawai'i Press
HONOLULU

Library of Congress Cataloging-in-Publication Data

Wichman, Frederick B.
  Nā pua aliʻi o kauaʻi : ruling chiefs of Kauaʻi / Frederick B. Wichman.
    p. cm.
  "A latitude 20 book."
  Includes bibliographical references and index.
  ISBN 0–8248–2587–X (hardcover : alk. paper) —
  ISBN 0–8248–2638–8 (pbk. : alk. paper)
    1. Hawaii—History—To 1893. 2. Hawaii—Kings and rulers.
I. Title. II. Title: Ruling chiefs of Kauaʻi.
  DU627.W53 2003
  996.9'02—dc21

                                    2002014101

Designed by Teresa Bonner

To my family, past, present, and future

CONTENTS

INTRODUCTION

POLYNESIAN HISTORY WAS PRESERVED WITHIN THE SONGS AND narratives recited in the formal setting of the high chief's court or in the informal setting of a family gathering. The chronology of these historical narratives was ordered by the genealogy of the high chief, which stretched back to the time when the gods walked the earth. The highest chiefs, the *pua ali'i,* the brightest flowers of royalty, were living gods on earth. Their genealogies, memorized and recited on significant occasions, proved their descent from Kāne, Lono, Kū, and Kanaloa, the four great gods of Polynesia.

In these legends, passed intact from generation to generation, were answers to the questions Who are we? Where did we come from? Who are our ancestors, and what did they do? What lessons can we learn from their conduct? Their lives, then and now, were held up as models of proper behavior and actions.

There are only fragments left of nearly two thousand years of the history of the Polynesian men and women who inhabited the island of Kaua'i before the arrival of Captain James Cook in 1778. Even these fragments are splintered, buried in out-of-print books, in public and private archives and notebooks, and frequently as part of the stories of other islands.

That these fragments exist at all is due to the determined efforts

x

of certain collectors in the nineteenth century to preserve an already dying culture.

Beginning in the 1830s, students of Maui's Lahainaluna School were asked to seek out, during their vacations, the oldest men and women on their island, ask them of the ancient ways, and write down the answers. Thus David Malo and Samuel Kamakau, most famously, began collecting information and stories and are today primary sources of pre-contact Hawaiian culture.

They were followed by Abraham Fornander, who amassed six volumes of legends and chants and began a history of the pre-contact Hawaiian islands. His Majesty King Kalākaua urged the compilation of genealogies and chants and himself oversaw a book of legends. There were others who wrote down what they remembered of the stories told by their grandparents that appeared in Hawaiian-language newspapers.

All references to the Kaua'i *ali'i nui* (paramount chiefs), wherever found, are here brought together and connected to the genealogy of those chiefs, placing them in chronological order. These histories are also narratives of great voyagers, bitter wars, heroes of gigantic size, and passionate romances that stir both heart and imagination. The reigns of some *ali'i nui* were so peaceful that no events were recorded for posterity. Other reigns were filled with stirring events and gave rise to lengthy reports.

There is no way to prove whether these stories reflect a factual history. These stories of the *pua ali'i o Kaua'i*, the royal flowers of Kaua'i, are the history as handed down from one generation to the next since ancient times, the report of thousands of years. Since only these stories survive, as shaped by the *haku mele* (poets) and *haku ka'ao* (storytellers), it is fitting that these legends are gathered here as stories that illuminate a history, not accurate in every detail of fact, not complete, yet all there is.

I

KINOHI LOA
The Beginning

THE SUN RISES AND SETS OVER KAUA'I, GENTLE TIDES RISE AND fall, the moon waxes and wanes, rain falls and the sun shines, and one day slips quietly into the next with little change. Men and women are born and die, and the passing of time in the days of ancient Kaua'i was recalled by reciting the genealogy of *nā ali'i nui* (paramount chiefs) in order from the first man, Kumu-honua, and first woman, Lalo-honua, through all their descendants down to the *ali'i nui* who ruled the people at the moment these genealogies were chanted.

These *pua ali'i*, exalted men and women, chiefs and descendants of chiefs, owned a genealogy that reached unbroken *mai ka pō mai* (from the time of darkness) to the present. These chiefs were considered to be directly descended from the gods themselves, from Kū, Kāne, Kanaloa, and Lono. These gods had created the first man and woman at 'Aliō, the beach beside the mouth of the mighty Wailua river. Thus the genealogy of a chief that began with Kumu-honua and continued unbroken from the time of darkness proved that he or she was sacred, godlike, invested with the power of life and death and ruled as the child of the gods.

There were several such genealogies, but the one most often chanted for Kaua'i's *pua ali'i* was the Kumu-honua genealogy.

2

The first thirty-six generations from Kumu-honua to Papa represent almost a thousand years of history. Even the best trained oral historian could not retain such massive history and genealogy, and there was no writing, therefore no books, in which this knowledge could be stored. Only a handful of legends recounting the adventures of certain *ali'i nui* have come down to us from that early time: Kini-lau-a-Mano, the great lover who ventured from island to island seeking new wives; Ke-ao-melemele, princess of the golden cloud in whose time the study of clouds as navigational aids and as clues to the future was first codified; Nu'u, who survived the great flood; and Hawai'i-loa, great voyager and discoverer of new stars and planets by which to navigate.

The legends of these chiefs and chiefesses are more than the mere retelling of heroic adventures. They are also a vast storehouse of accumulated information, of social mores with examples of good and bad behavior, and a general illustration of the best way to go about the business of living. They are also the way the Polynesians who settled and were born and died on Kaua'i tracked the passage of time and the chronology of their history.

The genealogy of Kumu-honua and his wife, Lalo-honua, continues for thirty-six generations until the birth of Papa. Her story indicates that she was the first to lead her people into the great unknown of the Pacific Ocean and was the mother of all Polynesians. Later genealogists turned her into Papa, the Earth Mother, goddess of all the life-giving land, and changed her husband, Wākea, into the Sky Father, god of all that belongs to the heavens. It was a new beginning, an anchor point from which all subsequent generations descended.

With Papa and Wākea, the history of Polynesia and of the island of Kaua'i begins. Behind them lay the mythical beginnings of the Polynesian people complete with the knowledge and culture accumulated over thousands of years. Ke-ao-melemele's clouds and Hawai'i-loa's navigational stars filled them with confidence that any islands to the east could be found and settled, and the way between the old and new homelands could be fixed in navigational lore.

Papa was a chiefess of high rank. It is not known where she lived, perhaps on Tonga or Samoa or even Fiji. She was, it is said, a handsome woman, noted in particular for her skill in fishing for *pāpa'i* (crab), which she served raw with *limu* (seaweed).

Wākea, who was born on an island to the west, was the second son of Kahiko and Kū-pūlana-kehau. When his older brother Līhau-'ula inherited Kahiko's land, Līhau-'ula wanted to get rid of the threat he saw in Wākea. His counselor tried to talk him out of it, saying, "Don't let us go to war with Wākea at this time. We shall be defeated by him."

Līhau-'ula had a large force of men under his control while Wākea had few, and so Līhau-'ula went to war. He lost his life, and the kingdom went to Wākea.

Immediately, Chief Kāne-ia-kumu-honua challenged him for the leadership. Their armies fought, and Wākea and his men were driven into the sea. There they bobbed in the ocean waves, without food or shelter, too far from friendly land to swim ashore.

Wākea turned to Komo-'awa, his *kahuna pule* (priest), and said, "What shall we do to save our lives?"

"Build a *heiau* (place of worship) and pray to the gods," Komo-'awa replied.

Wākea demanded to know how they could accomplish such a thing, since there was no wood floating nearby to make a raft much less a place of worship, and there were no pigs swimming with them to offer as sacrifice.

Komo-'awa said, "Lift up your right hand and form the hollow of your hand into a cup by lifting up your fingers." Wākea did so. "Now form the fingers of your left hand into a cone and put the fingertips into the hollow of your right hand." Wākea obeyed. "This is the *heiau*," Komo-'awa said. "All we need now are prayers." Komo-'awa began to chant.

Wākea and his warriors gathered close to listen to the prayers. When Komo-'awa finished, he said, "We are saved. Let us swim ashore."

The warriors did not doubt the word of their priest and followed Wākea ashore. In fury they engaged the enemy in battle and defeated Kāne-ia-kumu-honua. Then Wākea looked about for a suitable wife.

The legends that remain are silent concerning how Wākea and Papa met or where they lived. They did, however, produce a daughter, Ho'ohoku-i-ka-lani. She became a very lovely young woman. Wākea fell in love with her and desired to sleep with her. He knew Papa would be jealous and would not like the idea of him sleeping with his own daughter. Wākea tried to find a way to keep Papa from finding out. Once again he turned to Komo-'awa, his *kahuna pule*.

"If you desire your daughter," Komo-'awa said, "then you must

4

declare certain nights of the month *kapu* (taboo) when you must be separated from Papa. I will tell Papa that this is the will of the gods, and she will pay strict attention to it since it comes from the gods. You must also forbid men and women from eating together, as well as restricting certain foods from being eaten by women."

In this way and for this reason, Wākea began the tradition of four nights of prayer each month. No longer were men and women to eat together, and women could no longer eat pork, *niu aleleo* (coconuts with brown husks), and *niu hiwa* (coconuts with green husks). Women could no longer eat *manō* (shark), *ulua* (jackfish), *honu* (turtle), *honu'ea* (hawksbill turtle), or red fish such as *kūmū* (goatfish). They were also restricted to eating only two varieties of banana, the *mai'a iho lena* and *mai'a pōpō'ulu*.

These laws were put in place, and on the first *kapu* night, Wākea slept with his daughter, and Papa did not know it.

The second time, however, Wākea overslept. Komo-'awa, who had been keeping a lookout, chanted to awaken him.

Moku ka pawa,	The predawn darkness is breaking,
Lele ka hoku.	The morning star appears.
Haule ka lani,	Fallen is the chief,
Moakaka i ke ao malamalama.	Visible in the light of day.
Ala mai, ua ao e!	Awake, day has come!

Still, Wākea did not hear. After the sun rose, Wākea wrapped the bedsheet around him and dashed for the men's eating house. Papa saw him, found Ho'ohoku-i-ka-lani in the sleeping house from which Wākea had run and, furious, confronted Wākea. The two quarreled. It ended when Wākea spat in Papa's face, thus formally divorcing her.

Papa sailed to Tahiti where she took a new husband. She is said to have died and to have been buried in Tahiti. It is also said she returned to Wākea and bore him at least one more child, Ka-māwae-lua-lani-moku.

Wākea, freed of his jealous wife, continued his relationship with his daughter. Ho'ohoku-i-ka-lani's first child was premature. He was given the name Hāloa-naka. He did not live long, and his body was buried beside the house. From this burial place grew a *kalo* (taro) which became the staple food of Polynesia. Wākea named the leaf of this plant *lau kapalili* (quivering leaf) and the stem *hāloa* (long stem). Thus it was that the *kalo* plant was considered semi-sacred and life-giving, worthy of much respect and care.

Ho'ohoku-i-ka-lani gave birth to another son whom they named Hāloa after his dead brother. From Hāloa, it is said, descend all the Polynesians. Kaua'i historians claim that a younger brother of Hāloa discovered and settled this island.

This was Chief Ka-māwae-lua-lani-moku, son of Papa and Wākea, who traveled to this island with his wife, Kahiki-lau-lani, and her two paddlers Kō-nihinihi and Kō-nahenahe. Because of his good deeds, the great number of his descendants, and the prosperity of his reign, people began to call the island Kau-a'i (*"Place of Abundance"*).

Kau-a'i also means "to place around the neck," referring to the fact that only the most favored children were carried seated on the necks of their parents, the way Wākea carried his daughter Ho'o-hoku-i-ka-lani as an infant.

Kaua'i is also the name of the youngest son of ancient voyager Hawai'i-loa. His wife was Wai-'ale'ale, and her name was given to the lake beside the highest peak of the island. The word *Kaua'i* itself is older than Hawai'i-loa; its true meaning is lost in the mists of the cosmic night from which Kaua'i's ruling chiefs descended.

Kū'alu-nui-kini-akua

Whether Ka-māwae-lua-lani-moku and Kahiki-lau-lani ever lived on Kaua'i is unknown. It is more certain that one day, not too many generations after Papa and well before the descendants of Nana'ulu came to Kaua'i, a voyaging canoe commanded by Kū'alu-nui-kini-akua approached the island from the west. Nothing is known of him except his name and that he had a son Kū'alu-nui-paukū-moku-moku and a counselor named Pi'i-ali'i. The genealogy of the first Kaua'i settlers is broken, for they lost their lands and identity after a long war to new, vigorous, and more warlike adventurers. Only a few names remain of these first settlers and their descendants, the most famous connected to two almost mythical groups of people, the Menehune and the Mū.

Kū'alu-nui-kini-akua stepped ashore at the mouth of the Waimea river. It was an ideal place. There was abundant water from the swift rivers and streams that flowed within a protected canyon complex. The climate was warm and dry, useful for people who wore clothes of beaten bark. The area was cooled by Wai-paoa (*"Scooped Water"*),

6

a daytime breeze from the sea, and Wai-pa'ū ("*Water Drenched*") from the mountains at night. There was good soil within the canyon valleys behind the cliff that blocked easy access into the interior. The cliff they named Pali-uli after an ancient homeland and lost paradise. Taro could easily be grown in fields that took water from the river upstream, fed by ditches to each connected *lo'i* (taro patch) before returning the water to the river. Sweet potatoes and yams grew well, and early Western visitors spoke of fourteen-pound yams.

To the west were the marshes and ponds of Mānā, home of countless edible birds. The shallow channel between Waimea and Ni'ihau was home to such fishes as the *ulua* (jackfish), *mahimahi* (dolphin), *ono* (mackerel), and *a'u* (marlin), all large enough to feed many people. In addition, there were the reef fish, sea urchins, squid, and seaweeds.

The river itself was generous in its gift of *'o'opu* (goby). Once a year the spawn of the *'o'opu (hinana)* swam down the rivers to the sea in such numbers that they touched the skin of anyone entering the water. *Hinana* were only one or two inches in length and were easily netted. They quickly became a favorite food. Better yet, after a season in the ocean the *hinana* returned as adult *'o'opu* to their spawning grounds, and their life cycle began again.

In addition, these first settlers found a native tree they named *waimea*, which had a bark that could be used to make *kapa* (cloth). Cloth made from *waimea* was coarse and heavy compared to that made from *wauke* (mulberry). It was durable if kept dry but tore like paper when wet. For these settlers it served a purpose until such time as the slips of *wauke* they had brought with them could be planted and multiplied to give them enough cloth for their clothes and bedding.

From the beginning the Kaua'i people developed unique tools never seen on other islands. These included *pōhaku ku'i poi* (ring and stirrup pounders), double-grooved stone club heads, and a broad anvil for beating *kapa*. They learned how to weave intricately designed mats of *makaloa* (sedge) so soft it could be used for clothing. They discovered a method for decorating their *ipu* (bottle gourds), which they used as containers for food and water. They strung the tiny seashells found on the beaches into necklaces. Brightly feathered birds abounded from seashore to mountaintop, and their feathers were collected and woven into wreaths, capes, and helmets. Throughout their entire history, the people of Kaua'i created things of beauty from even the most ordinary objects.

The twenty-nine or so plants essential to life that had been collected over the centuries were planted and thrived. Pi'i-ali'i, Kū'alu-nui-kini-akua's *kālaimoku* (chief counselor) brought a species of taro called Pi'i-ali'i, which is still grown on Kaua'i. In later days it was kept for the use of the *ali'i* and as a proper offering to the gods.

As the population increased, settlements spread inward into Waimea canyon and its side canyons, into the valleys of Nāpali, along the southern coast to Koloa and northward to Wailua and Hanalei. Ni'ihau was included as an integral part of the island, inhabited after rain fell and deserted during times of drought.

Kū'alu-nui-paukū-mokumoku

Soon after he became ruling chief, Kū'alu-nui-paukū-mokumoku's wife died in what at first seemed to be an accident. After several young men who might possibly have become his heir also died, he suspected that his *kahuna nui* (high priest) was involved, for he knew the *kahuna* wanted to return to their homeland. The *kahuna* and his followers were tired of the hardscrabble life, without the comforts of home.

The fact that Kū'alu-nui-paukū-mokumoku was losing his heirs one after another, the *kahuna nui* said, was a sign of godly displeasure that they yet remained on Kaua'i. Suspecting a personal motive in this, Kū'alu-nui-paukū-mokumoku refused to leave Kaua'i.

Kū'alu-nui-paukū-mokumoku needed an heir if the colony on Kaua'i was to survive. He would need to marry again and devise a way to keep her and her child alive until that child reached adulthood. The chief and Pi'i, his right-hand man (*kālaimoku*) and son of his father's counselor, crafted a plan. Kū'alu-nui-paukū-mokumoku married Kahāpula, a chiefess who had been born on the slopes of Pe'ape'a peak overlooking Hanapēpē valley. When she became pregnant, Kū'alu-nui-paukū-mokumoku publicly accused Pi'i of being the father of the child and banished both of them to Moku-one, a remote valley in the upper Waimea canyon. Before they left, Kū'alu-nui-paukū-mokumoku gave Kahāpula a red *malo* (loincloth) and a *lei 'ōpu'u* (whale tooth pendant on a cord of human hair), emblems that only the high chief could wear, and told her to have their son bring these to him as proof of his identity when he came of age. He also gave her a nut from a *kukui* tree that he asked her to plant beside her new house. Then Kū'alu-nui-paukū-mokumoku waited until his son grew into adulthood.

Pi'i led Kahāpula into Moku-one valley and saw that she had a home built on the banks of a stream, which eventually was named Māhu-o-Ola (*"Ola's stream"*). She planted the *kukui* nut beside her new home. After Kahāpula gave birth to a boy, he and the *kukui* tree grew up far from the suspicious eyes of the *kahuna nui.* Pi'i taught him the skills of a warrior and of a statesman, and his mother taught him the chants and genealogy of his ancestors. He was a very mischievous boy and was constantly in trouble.

When Kū'alu-nui-paukū-mokumoku judged the boy had become a youth, he issued an order demanding that everyone help build a temple *(heiau)* to celebrate the success of their new settlement. On a ridge above Wai'awa valley, a *heiau* was built of natural waterworn reddish lava stone brought from the stream bed a hundred feet below. They paved the *heiau* floor with coral brought from the beach. The high priest insisted on a human sacrifice at the opening ceremony.

To have enough food on hand for the celebration, Kū'alu-nui-paukū-mokumoku ordered his people to build a bamboo *kahe* (trap) to catch the *'o'opu* fish living in the white waters of upper Waimea river. The *kahuna nui* ordered that no one was to touch the trap until the *kahuna* himself had removed the *kapu* he had laid on it. Kahāpula's son saw the *kahe* and the large number of *'o'opu* caught in it and, disregarding this *kapu*, helped himself freely to the fish. He was reported to the *kahuna,* who was delighted to have found a human sacrifice for the newly built *heiau*. The youth was taken to Wai'awa and kept prisoner until the time came to sacrifice him.

Kahāpula heard of her son's capture and asked Pi'i what to do. He told her, "Take your son to Kū'alu-nui-paukū-mokumoku dressed in the *malo* and *lei 'ōpu'u* as he requested. Pick six *kukui* nuts from the tree growing beside your house. You must walk to Wai'awa, and as you go you must toss the six nuts into the air and catch them. If you drop one, your child will die. If you catch all, his life will be spared."

Kahāpula bundled up the royal tokens, picked six *kukui* nuts, and began her long walk, juggling the nuts as she went.

The path she had to follow was rocky, rutted, treacherous underfoot, and there were many streams and rivers to cross. The inhabitants of Moku-one, without a word to one another, all went before her, clearing the path of any rocks on which she might stumble, and laying down a matting of grass for easier walking. They filled in fords across each stream so she would not slip on mossy rocks. They helped her by chanting in a steady rhythm so that her feet, as in a *hula*, moved in a steady beat.

So she went, gathering more and more people who willingly cleared her path until at last she reached Wai'awa. She had no trouble finding her son and untied his ropes. Even the guards had simply stepped aside and watched as she helped her boy put on the red *malo* and fastened the *lei 'ōpu'u* around his neck. When the priests came for him, they did not find a cowering captive but instead a warrior in full royal regalia.

As soon as the young captive entered the *heiau*, he claimed his heritage as Kū'alu-nui-paukū-mokumoku's son. The *kahuna nui*, immediately realizing the loss of his hopes, threw his short spear in an attempt to kill the youth. The young man contemptuously brushed the spear aside. The *kahuna*, having defiled the *heiau* precinct, stabbed himself and fell onto the altar, thus inadvertently becoming the first human sacrifice noted in Kaua'i legends.

Kū'alu-nui-paukū-mokumoku named his son Ola (*"Life"*) and the *heiau* Hau-ola (*"Live offering"* or *"Dew of life"*). He also asked Kahāpula to return to their home in Waimea, but she refused, having become used to life in her remote valley. From time to time Kū'alu-nui-paukū-mokumoku would visit her but she never again lived beside the sea.

The Menehune

While waiting for his son to be born, Kū'alu-nui-paukū-mokumoku sent back to his homeland for the Menehune who were masters of stonework and engineering. Under Kū'alu-nui-paukū-mokumoku, the Menehune built many *heiau*, fishponds, and irrigation systems for wetland farming.

The Menehune were an energetic, broad-shouldered, and muscular people. They were organized in divisions based upon their skills and duties, and they were completely obedient to their leaders. There were twenty divisions of men and eight of women. They worked as a team, and if a project was interrupted for any reason, they abandoned it and never returned to finish it. Their greatest demand regarding payment was that each of them should receive exactly the same amount of food as any of the others, be it only one shrimp. Their preferred living area was on the ridge between Wainiha and Lumahaʻi valleys.

The Menehune built Malae *heiau* on the banks of the Wailua river. Its outside walls are 273 feet long by 324 feet wide. The walls were seven to ten feet high and eight feet wide at the top, thirteen feet at the base. A ledge six feet wide and two feet above the ground ran all around the inside of these walls. People sat here during the ceremonies. It is the largest place of worship ever built on Kauaʻi. Within its walls once lived Hina-hau-kaekae who turned herself into the first *hau* tree to meet the needs of the desperate people she met one fateful day.

On the ridge on the opposite shore of Wailua river, the Menehune built Poli-ʻahu *heiau*. This was a *heiau* paved with large flat lava stones. It is roughly rectangular, 242 feet long and 165 feet wide. There was a terrace on the west end with the unusual feature of a row of stones placed on edge. The *kahuna nui* of Poli-ʻahu communicated with the *kahuna* of Malae by striking the *pōhaku kani* (bell stone), a large rock that produced a clear bell-like sound when struck with the stalk of a *ti* plant. The sound could be heard a mile away.

ʻAlekoko fishpond in Hulā-ʻia river was begun but never finished. The pond is created by a dirt wall more than 900 yards long that cuts off a meander of the river. The wall was covered with stone facing. It was built at the request of the chief ʻAlekoko and his sister Hāhālua who each wanted a fishpond. The Menehune agreed, laying down only one stipulation: Neither should look out of their houses during the night of construction. Hāhālua contented herself with imagining the succulent fish she would eat from her own fishpond and refused to look out. Her brother, however, tormented all night long by the sound of humming voices, finally poked a hole through his thatch wall and peered out. Immediately, the Menehune dropped the stones they were holding and washed their bleeding hands in the water, hence giving the fishpond its name, ʻAlekoko (*Bloody Ripples*).

Ola

When Ola succeeded his father as ruler, he first wanted to enlarge the farming area of Waimea. The *makai* (seaward) portion between the ridges and the ocean would be rich farmland if it could be irrigated. The land was too far above the river level, for the farmers of that time only knew how to make water flow by gravity. *Mauka* (toward the mountain), Pali-uli cliff blocked access to the river. To get water to flow around Pali-uli, an irrigation *'auwai* (channel) would have to be constructed twenty feet above the river's surface, a seemingly impossible feat. Ola sent his counselor Pi'i to ask the Menehune if they could build such an *'auwai*.

The Menehune leader, Papa-enaena, studied the lay of the land and decided that indeed such an *'auwai* could be built. He demanded that there should be no noise on the night they were working—no roosters crowing, no children crying, no dogs yipping, no people whispering, complete silence except the noises the Menehune themselves would be making. At dawn, as they filed back to their mountain home, each Menehune must receive an equal amount of the same food. In addition, Papa-enaena said, Ola must offer the proper prayers to the gods, and then he was to lie down in the place where they would end their *'auwai*. There Papa-enaena would make him sleep. If all had been properly done, Ola would awaken when the waters poured over him, but if the project was unfinished because of forbidden noises, dawn came too soon, or prayers were incorrectly said, Ola would not awaken and would drown. Ola agreed, and on the appointed night the Menehune began their work.

The Menehune solved the problem caused by Pali-uli by anchoring a wall in the riverbed itself and building it up against the cliff. They used cut stone blocks that were squared off. Some of these stones are five feet long, three feet wide, and three feet deep and came from a quarry several miles away on the other side of the river. Some blocks are jointed, a peg carved from one block fits a hole drilled in another.

By dawn the *'auwai* was finished. Papa-enaena woke Ola as the first flow of water drenched him. This channel and the area it waters is still known as Kīkī-a-Ola (*Container [acquired] by Ola*).

Pi'i first tried to feed each Menehune one *moi* (threadfish), but he ran out before each Menehune got one. The Menehune agreed to give him one more day to gather enough food, and he ordered every shrimp that could be found in the streams to be gathered. Place names recall this event: Ala-pi'i (*Pi'i's Road*), Hali-'ōpae (*Fetched Shrimp*), and 'Ōpae-pi'i (*Pi'i's Shrimp*). That following night, each Menehune received one shrimp as payment and was content. The hill where this payment took place is still called Pu'u-'ōpae (*Shrimp Hill*).

Ola then began to explore the mountainous regions. He found that Puʻu-kāpele, 3,662 feet above the sea, had perfect conditions for the growing of *koa* and *koaiʻe* trees. These produced a hardwood that was used to carve calabashes, idols, paddles, and the blunt-bladed *ōʻō* (farmer's digging tool). Here he built a small village that became the home of canoe builders. They farmed *koa* trees, cutting off side branches so that the trunk would grow without curves or twists up to 120 feet tall and have no flaws in it.

When a chief desired a new canoe, the *kahuna kālai waʻa* (master canoe carver) searched for a suitable tree. Once felled, the trunk was hewed out and then hauled under the supervision of the *kahuna pale waʻa* (expert in moving canoes) to a shed on the beach where it was finished. On a nearby knoll, Ola built Hālau-a-Ola (*Ola's Shed*), a place of refuge for anyone who had broken a *kapu*.

In addition, Ola is said to have built the three-stepped *heiau* of Ahu-loulu (*Loulu Palm Shrine*) at the foot of Puʻu-kāpele crater. The *loulu* is a native fan palm whose fronds are used to thatch a *heiau* built specifically for the prevention of epidemics, famine, or destruction. *Loulu* is the name, also, of a series of long rituals including the consecration of a temple by redecorating certain images with feathers (*kauila nui*), the process of obtaining the logs of *ʻōhiʻa* trees for making images of the gods (*haku ʻōhiʻa*), prayer committed to memory and recited in unison (*kuili*), as well as a rite at the end of *kapu loulu* rituals during which chiefs sat without shifting positions while a *kahuna* prayed for as long as an hour (*hono*).

Ola and the Menehune found that the center of the island was dominated by a huge swamp, the Alakaʻi. The swamp is a sea of water, grass, shrub-covered humps, and mud. Travelers can quickly become disoriented and lose their way in a matter of moments. Fog, mist, and heavy rains can obscure everything so that travelers can hardly see someone standing only two feet away. It is primeval, fascinating, and dangerous. Hummocks of dwarf shrubbery float on the surface of the water, looking like solid land when in reality they are only water and mud. An unwary traveler dumped into the bog emerges dyed a golden brown from the mud. Ola marked a trail through the swamp, skirting bogs that could be either ankle or shoulder deep, depending on the recent rainfall.

Along one nasty stretch, the Menehune constructed Ka-lāʻau-kipapa-a-Ola (*Wooden pavement of Ola*). This was a corduroy path consisting of logs of *hapuʻu* (tree fern) laid side by side across this very muddy and wet place. The *hapu'u* sprouted, and the path became bordered by a grove of tree fern, their lacy fronds bending in the wind and rain.

Many years later Menehune Queen Mōhihi, seeing that her men were marrying Hawaiian women, decided to take her people back to their original homeland. The Menehune gathered in the mountains and marched along the edge of the Nāpali valleys until they reached the plains of Hā'ena. There they entered their canoes and sailed away, leaving only their prodigious stone ruins, their place names, and a few of their stories behind.

Like his ancestor Hawai'i-loa, Ola also contended with cannibalism. For several nights in a row, Ola and Pi'i noticed a bonfire flickering on the shores of Ni'ihau where no one lived. He asked his friend Ka-hao-o-ka-moku, who was about to set off on a fishing expedition to Ka'ula islet, to stop by Ni'ihau and find out who was there. Two days later Kāne-'opa, the head *lawai'a* (fisherman) of the expedition, returned alone with a harrowing tale. As they landed on Ni'ihau, the fishing party had been greeted by a man who offered them food, shelter, and women. This unknown man had then shown them into a house where, tired from fishing, one by one they fell asleep, all except Kāne-'opa who was suspicious by nature and who had not liked the stranger's manner.

In the dark of night, Kāne-'opa heard the stranger, whose name was Hana-au-moe, at the door, whispering:

Kahea ana o Hanaaumoe, moe ea?	Greetings from Hana-au-moe, are you asleep?
Halahala kau e,	Piled on one another,
Halahala kau e,	Scattered here and there,
Ua moe oukou?	Are you all asleep?

Kāne-'opa immediately replied, "We are not asleep. We are still awake waiting for the food and our wives."

Once Hana-au-moe left again, Kāne-'opa, afraid he would fall asleep, dug a hole under the doorway stone and hid himself there. Once again Hana-au-moe repeated his call but no one answered this time. Hana-au-moe whispered, "You shall surely be killed. Why didn't you sleep on Kaua'i instead of coming and sleeping on this island? You are as good as dead; there is no escape. Your flesh, your bones, your bowels, your blood, your eyes, all will be eaten up." There was a rush of men through the doorway, and all the Kaua'i men were killed except Kāne-'opa who remained hidden. The unsuspecting fishermen were eaten where they died.

At dawn, Kāne-'opa escaped with the dreadful news. Ola and Pi'i immediately made preparations. At dusk they arrived on Ni'ihau where Hana-au-moe greeted them, offering them food and wives. As soon as he had scurried off, Ola and Pi'i placed wooden idols within the house. Then they concealed themselves in the hole beneath the door sill. When Hana-au-moe returned, he saw the large staring eyes of the wide-awake Kaua'i men gleaming in the darkness and went away again. As soon as he left, Ola and Ki'i lay the images down. When Hana-au-moe returned, there was no answer to his whisper and, with high hopes of a full belly, he brought back his companions. They rushed into the house, clubbed the sleeping men, and began to eat.

"'O'ole'a (Oh, how tough)!" cried one of the cannibals when he broke a tooth on a wooden idol. The others hardly had time to remark on the toughness of Kaua'i men when Ola and Pi'i were upon them and slaughtered them. Then Ola set the house on fire, and Ni'ihau was free of this cannibal group.

No mention of Ola's marriage or direct descendants has survived.

Ka-lā-kāne-hina

Sometime after Ola, Ka-lā-kāne-hina became *ali'i nui*. He lived at Lā'au-'ōkala, the eastern point of the Waimea river outlet. He married Lohipono, a chiefess of Wainiha valley. She left her infant son Kāne-a-Lohi with her brother Ka-lālā-pōpō'ulu, a birdcatcher who brought up his nephew in the mountains and trained him in the art of catching birds whose feathers were greatly prized.

Kāne-a-Lohi

Kāne-a-Lohi exasperated his uncle a great deal, for he refused to eat most kinds of food and always demanded the flesh of small birds. To feed this prodigious appetite, Ka-lālā-pōpō'ulu moved to the cliffs above Halulu waterfall on the very edge of the immense cliffs of Wai'ale'ale. Here *uwa'u* (dark-rumped petrel) nested in deep holes dug into the sides of the cliffs. Each morning the *uwa'u* flew out to sea, and each evening they flew home to their caves. The young, before they take on a heavy fishy flavor, are good to eat.

Uncle and nephew were not the only ones who liked the *uwa'u*. Ka-wai-pe'e, a giant from Pe'ape'a above Hanapēpē, took pleasure in destroying the nests of these birds, as well as killing the birds and flinging them away without eating them. He would station himself outside a bird cave and call "Pe'e, pe'e, pe'e!" When the birds answered him, he would reach into the hole and kill the birds.

This was intolerable to young Kāne-a-Lohi. The next time that the giant showed up in the area, Kāne-a-Lohi caught an *uwa'u* and tied a cord to its leg. He dug a deep hole, placed his uncle Ka-lālā-pōpō'ulu way back in it, and told him to let the bird go out to the mouth of the hole. Then he was to hold on to the cord and keep the bird at the entrance while Kāne-a-Lohi hid outside.

When Ka-wai-pe'e heard the distressed bird calling, he came and reached out for the bird, but as he did, Ka-lālā-pōpō'ulu pulled on the cord and drew the bird in deeper. Ka-wai-pe'e kept reaching for the bird, and Ka-lālā-pōpō'ulu kept pulling it in deeper until Ka-wai-pe'e was stretched out flat on the ground and had actually stuck his head into the hole in his attempt to catch the bird. At that moment Kāne-a-Lohi leaped on him and killed him.

From then on, no one came to disturb uncle and nephew on the cliffs above Halulu waterfall until Ka-lā-kāne-hina, the Waimea chief, heard there were men in the mountains who were destroying the *uwa'u* birds. They were his favorite eating birds, and he had placed a *kapu* on them. He gathered a band of soldiers and went to kill the lawbreakers.

The next day, uncle and nephew were roasting their birds on a spit. They were camping in their usual place, an open meadow beside a sheet of open water at the eastern edge of Alaka'i swamp looking down into Wainiha valley. Kāne-a-Lohi noticed that the pond water was rippling, which only happened if the water was disturbed at the other end deep within the swamp. Kāne-a-Lohi realized somebody was coming their way and knew they had little time to eat. He told his uncle to tear the birds into chunks so they could eat and be ready to fight on a full stomach.

Uncle and nephew stationed themselves at the edge of the cliff where the path was so narrow that only one man at a time could walk it. As each of Ka-lā-kāne-hina's soldiers came, Kāne-a-Lohi pushed him over the cliff to his death.

When Ka-lā-kāne-hina saw what had happened to his army, he

called out, "Save me, in the name of your mother, Lohipono. I am your father."

Kāne-a-Lohi said, "If you had not given my mother's name, I would have killed you."

Ka-lā-kāne-hina then said he would return to Waimea and build a house for Kāne-a-Lohi where he could live and learn the skills needed to become the next *aliʻi nui*. Kāne-a-Lohi agreed.

Ka-lā-kāne-hina rushed back to Waimea and built a house. Once the walls were up, he dug a deep wide hole inside it. He planted the bottom of the pit with sharpened spears, ready to impale anyone who fell onto them. Then he covered this pit with a mat. He hoped the unwary youth would step on the mat and fall to his death.

When Kāne-a-Lohi stooped and peered into the house, he immediately suspected foul play. The chief and all his men were seated along the walls on the edge of the mat, an unusual arrangement, and the mat sagged a little in the middle. Kāne-a-Lohi poked his spear through the mat. When it went through easily, he jumped back and barred the doorway. In their rush to get to the door, Ka-lā-kāne-hina and his men fell into the hole themselves. Kāne-a-Lohi set the house on fire.

For a short time Kāne-a-Lohi became *aliʻi nui*. He married and had a son, but soon took his mother and his son Ka-lau-lehua back to the mountains he loved.

Ka-lau-lehua

Ka-lau-lehua in his turn became *aliʻi nui*. He had spent his childhood in the mountains near the shores of Wai-ʻaleʻale, a small oblong-shaped lake whose waters constantly are ruffled by the wind. He followed the little stream that flowed out of the lake and found it was the source of the Wainiha river. For a reason not mentioned in legend, Ka-lau-lehua wanted to dig a ditch leading from Wai-ʻaleʻale to the cliff's edge so the pond would also be the headwaters of Wailua river.

Ka-lau-lehua sailed to the mythical island of Kāne-huna-moku to fetch the Mū-ʻai-maiʻa (Banana-eating people). These people used the banana as their staple plant. They ate the fruit and used the leaves for clothing and thatching their houses.

Ka-lau-lehua, it is said, tricked seven Mū, four men and three women, into coming with him from their homeland of Kāne-huna-moku. They first lived in Honopū, one of the Nāpali valleys. Then Ka-lau-lehua moved them to the upper Wainiha valley and ordered them to dig the ditch he wanted. The Mū refused and asked to be returned home.

Ka-lau-lehua would not help them. Instead he imposed a *kapu* from Pōhaku-loa to a *heiau* named Ka-'awa-kō and on to the little valley of Ka-ua-i-ka-nanā, which encompassed much of the Alaka'i swamp. "All this land you may live in," he told them. "The rest of the land belongs to me, and you may not set foot in it. If any of you step onto my lands, you shall die." Ka-lau-lehua set up logs to mark the boundaries of the *kapu* land. Then he forgot about them.

Ka-'awa-kō, on one end of Wai'ale'ale lake, became the center of worship for the Mū. The *heiau* was a small rectangular structure about five by seven feet, with walls two feet high made of smooth lava slabs. It was a very sacred place, and it is still suggested that any-one traveling there should leave some offering. If an offering is not left, the mountain gods will become angry and cause the clouds and heavy rains to hide the trail back out of the swamp.

The Mū remained in Wainiha and became experts at building elaborate bamboo *kahe* (traps) to catch the 'o'opu fish that headed to the sea in summer freshets. They offered the first fish they caught in the *kahe* to the gods at Ka-'awa-kō. They planted bananas any-where they found a spot big enough to hold the plant. Slowly they began to grow in number.

In time they had the reputation of being a shy people who did not know how to use fire and dressed in banana leaves. Even though the Menehune lived in the same area, the Mū avoided them, too, and watched unhappily when the Menehune sailed away. The Mū had lost the knowledge of the stars that would lead them back to their former homeland.

Ka-iki-pa'a-nānea

Several generations later, Ka-iki-pa'a-nānea, in his turn, became the *ali'i nui* of Kaua'i. His headquarters was on the small plateau on the eastern side of the Waimea river mouth.

Ka-iki-pa'a-nānea had two major passions: sports and riddles. He was a champion wrestler and boxer who always tried to kill his oppo-nent. Everyone feared and hated him. In fact, only his personal ser-vant, Kūkae-ā, was ever in his company. Kūkae-ā was abused and mistreated but allowed to live since he handled all personal items, like tasting the food first and disposing of all intimate articles such as hair and fingernails that a sorcerer could use.

At night, for amusement, Ka-iki-pa'a-nānea would pose two riddles to an unsuspecting guest. The first riddle was

Kai a puni,	Plaited all around,
Kai a lalo,	Plaited to the bottom,
A koe koena.	Leaving an opening.

The second was

Kanaka i ku,	The men that stand,
Kanaka i moe,	The men that lie down,
Kanaka i pelupelu ia.	The men that are folded.

The loser, who was anyone Ka-iki-pa'a-nānea could trick into playing his game, was thrown into a pit filled with red-hot stones. Again, he quickly found that no one cared to play at riddles with him either.

Worst still, when every chiefess on Kaua'i refused to marry him after the death of his wife, Ka-iki-pa'a-nānea sent his messengers to O'ahu, ordering them to bring him a wife. They saw a lovely woman named Mākolea surfing at Waikīkī, kidnapped her from her surfboard, and took her back to Kaua'i. There she, too, refused to marry Ka-iki-pa'a-nānea. He locked her up until she would agree to his proposal, letting her out only to watch him at boxing and riddling.

Mākolea was the wife of Ke-paka-'ili-'ula, a warrior from Maui. Ke-paka-'ili-'ula sailed to Kaua'i to free his wife. He befriended Ka-iki-pa'a-nānea's servant, Kūkae-ā, treating him kindly for the first time in the servant's life. Kūkae-ā warned the Maui man of the boxing match that Ka-iki-pa'a-nānea would certainly demand, but Ke-paka-'ili-'ula said he would issue the first challenge himself. Then the servant warned him of the riddles and, in gratitude, revealed the answers: to the first, the answer was a house. "It is thatched all around, except for the doorway," he explained. "A house is thatched on all four of its walls. A house is thatched from the ridge of the roof to the ground. Only the door is left as an opening."

The answer to the second riddle was also a house. Kūkae-ā explained, "The men that stand are the posts set into the ground.

The men that lie down are the beams that connect the posts and the men that are folded are the pili grasses bent in two to make the bundles that thatch the house."

Armed with this information, Ke-paka-'ili-'ula challenged Ka-iki-pa'a-nānea to a boxing challenge, which the Maui warrior won after he had broken one of the long bones in Ka-iki-pa'a-nānea's arm. That night the Kaua'i chief posed his riddles, and Ke-paka-'ili-'ula, of course, answered both correctly. Then Ke-paka-'ili-'ula seized the cruel ruler, lifted him over his head, and tossed him into a firepit filled with red-hot stones.

Ka-iki-pa'a-nānea, preoccupied with riddles and athletics, had earlier allowed an ocean traveler from the Marquesas, Puna-nui-ka-ia-'āina, to settle with his entourage on the banks of the Wailua river where the Menehune had built their magnificent places of worship. Whatever Ka-iki-pa'a-nānea thought of the newcomers, he had no threatening warriors on shore to push the invaders back. The land was rich; it was not crowded. There was no reason why the newcomers shouldn't take over the lands that came to be called Puna.

There were now two chiefdoms, Puna and Kona, on Kaua'i. The seeds of future conflict were sown.

NĀ HOLOKAI
The Seafarers

MEANWHILE, FAR TO THE SOUTH OF KAUAʻI, OTHER ISLANDS OF Polynesia were being discovered and settled. Voyaging canoes crisscrossed the South Pacific as though the mighty ocean was as calm as a small pond on a windless day.

These canoes were double hulled. A *pola* (platform) between them supported a mast, a firepit, and a cabin for the chief. The hulls were twelve feet deep with ample room to store all the supplies for the voyage, as well as the seeds and slips of the twenty-nine plants that were the staples of their lives. These canoes were equipped with sails and oars. They were staffed with men and women undoubtedly chosen in the same manner that Kiʻi used when he chose companions for his sons Nanaʻulu and ʻUlu.

ʻUlu and Nanaʻulu

Thirteen generations, or more than three hundred years, after Papanui-hānau-moku and Wākea, a chief of Tahiti, Kiʻi, and his wife, Hina-kō-ʻula, became parents of two sons, Nanaʻulu and ʻUlu. When they were grown, Kiʻi asked his sons to go on voyages of discovery. All memory of the navigational signposts back to their original homeland had been forgotten. Two voyaging canoes were built and equipped with all the provisions needed for a long voyage. Now it was time to choose the crew.

Every chief and many commoners wanted to go with Nana'ulu and 'Ulu, but there was obviously room only for a limited number on board. In order to take the best, Ki'i ordered a series of tests. Only those who had successfully won a competition would be allowed to go.

The first contest was *hakoko* (wrestling). The chiefly warriors Makina and Opale stepped into a ring formed by spectators. As a preliminary, it was customary for opponents to insult each other, boasting to the audience that his opponent was so far beneath contempt that he only needed to make one move and the bout would be over.

Chief Makina chanted in a half-shouting, defiant tone and compared his opponent to the calm lagoon waters of Makavia, too flat and placid to make much of a foe unlike the breakers beyond the reef. Opale, not to be outdone, looked up into the sky, glanced along the sand as though searching for something, then chanted that he could see only a boastful little man with weak legs and arms and demanded to know when the warrior Makina would appear.

Both chiefs had now thoroughly worked up their anger. They stood face to face and, at the same moment, each made a sudden movement hoping to find the other off guard. They were well matched and soon only a glimpse of arms, legs, and writhing bodies could be seen through the dust. Then for long frozen moments, the two remained motionless, muscles straining to make the other give way. Doing his best to prevent Makina from knowing what he meant to do, Opale suddenly swept one foot against his foe's leg, hoping to throw him to the ground. But that briefest loosening of muscles had alerted Makina to his opponent's gambit and, even as Opale's foot struck him, Makina raised the unbalanced chief off the ground and spun him over his head while keeping his own balance with whirlwind motions. Then Makina threw Opale to the ground, where he lay unconscious for a moment. Makina had won a place in one of the canoes.

Another contest was *mokomoko* (boxing). The opponents clenched their fists and struck each other directly upon the knuckles. The game usually ended with a broken arm, and he who was still on his feet was declared the winner.

Even after these two contests had eliminated half the chiefs by the end of the day, there were still too many to fit into the canoes. Ki'i declared that the following day would see a contest of surfboarding. The breakers were large and smooth. A lesser chief, Vai-ta-piha, caught a huge comber and, leaping to his feet, was having a spectacular ride to shore. Then, in front of Vai-ta-piha, another surfer was thrown from his board, hit his head and began sinking into the sea. Vai-ta-piha dove off his board, caught the unconscious chief, regained his board and his feet and, holding his friend in his arms, coasted onto the sand. His bravery and skill earned him a place in a canoe.

Next came *hōlua* (sled racing), sliding down a steep prepared course on eight-inch–wide sleds. The most daring were able to stand, no easy thing to do. The man who made the longest run won.

There were still too many chiefs to fit into the canoes. Ki'i ordered a long, smooth path be made and beaten down until it was hard. Then each man would throw a heavy javelin, the longest throw winning.

Next came *'ulu maika* (bowling), but Nana'ulu made this more difficult. Using the same course as the javelin throw, at the other end Nana'ulu set up two sticks through which the *maika,* a polished stone about two inches thick and a foot and a half in circumference, had to pass. The stone had to roll on its side through the two sticks and strike a third stick several yards beyond.

Finally there was the spear-catching contest. Six spears were thrown at a chief by six other chiefs about sixty feet away. The lone chief had to catch, dodge or deflect all of these spears as they hurtled toward him.

When the contests were over, the successful chiefs and their wives were invited by Ki'i to take their places aboard one of the two canoes.

Meantime the commoners had been exhibiting their skills, also seeking a place in the canoes. Among them were canoe makers, masters of carving and lashing, house builders, and expert fishermen skilled in the use of lures and nets. Those chosen became the oarsmen. Their wives, too, were invited on board.

Thus each canoe was filled with strong, agile, intelligent men and women capable of withstanding the dangers of the sea and the rigors of settling a new land. Nana'ulu sailed north in his canoe named Manō-nui (*Great Shark*) and found the islands of Hawai'i. The way from Hawai'i to Tahiti was charted. Voyagers came in increasing numbers.

Meanwhile the descendants of 'Ulu spread out over the South Pacific. Among them were extraordinary people who lived such wonderful adventures that storytellers had rich material to develop into entertaining sagas.

There was Māui-kiʻikiʻi who snared the sun to make it go slower so his mother had time to dry her tapa, and who forced the secret of fire from the ʻalae birds so his mother could eat cooked food.

ʻAikanaka-a-Makoʻo lived with Hina-hānai-a-ka-mālama, who gave birth to twins, Puna and Hema. She grew so tired of cleaning up after their infant messes that she left them and climbed into the moon where she may still be seen beating her tapa in peace.

Her son Hema went to search for a birth present for his son Kahaʻi and never came back. In his turn, Kahaʻi set out to get a birth present for his son Wahieloa as well as look for his father, and he, too, never returned. The same thing happened to Wahieloa. It fell to the fourth generation in the person of Laka to remedy the situation. He got the Menehune to build him a strong voyaging canoe, obtained from his grandmother secrets and weapons to overcome the dangers that had beset his father, grandfather, and great-grandfather, and set out on an adventure-filled voyage. He found all three of his immediate ancestors and brought them triumphantly home.

There were so many astonishing ancestors like these that the genealogists added them all into the 'Ulu genealogy. Today there seems no way to reconcile the short Nanaʻulu and very long 'Ulu genealogies.

Two voyaging canoes set out from Tahiti fifteen generations after Nanaʻulu and arrived on Oʻahu and Kauaʻi. Maweke and Pau-makua settled peacefully on Oʻahu and quickly became ruling chiefs of a district of that island.

At the same time, Puna-nui-ka-ia-ʻāina, whose genealogy has not survived, arrived on Kauaʻi, having come, most likely, from the Marquesas Islands.

Puna-nui-ka-ia-ʻāina

Puna-nui-ka-ia-ʻāina arrived when the chief with the deadly riddles, Ka-iki-paʻa-nānea, was ruler of Waimea. The newcomer chose to settle along the banks of the Wailua river. This land came to be called Puna.

There were now two chiefdoms on Kauaʻi, Puna and Kona.

Puna-kai-'olohia

Puna-kai-'olohia followed his father, Puna-nui-ka-ia-'āina, as leader of his people along the banks of the broad Wailua. Nothing is known of him or his reign, except that he had a son.

Puna-'ai-koā-i'i

According to King Kalākaua, as quoted from his book, *The Legends and Myths of Hawaii:* "Puna, the governing *alii* [sic] of the island, held his court [at Wailua], surrounded by the chiefs of his family and a large number of retainers. Puna was one of the most popular rulers in the group, and, strict as he may have been in the exercise of his prerogatives, was always merciful in dealing with offenses thoughtlessly or ignorantly committed. He would pardon the humble laborer who might inadvertently cross his shadow or violate a *tabu*, but never the chief who deliberately trespassed upon his privileges or withheld a courtesy due to one of his rank. His disposition was naturally warlike, but as the condition of the island was peaceful, and military force was seldom required except in repelling the occasional plundering raids from the other islands, he kept alive the martial spirit of his chiefs and subjects by frequent sham fights, marine drills, and the encouragement of athletic games and friendly contests at arms, in which he himself sometimes took part. Feasting and dancing usually followed these warlike pastimes, and the result was that the court of Puna became somewhat noted for the chivalry of its chiefs and the splendor of its entertainments."

Puna-'ai-koā-i'i had only one child, his daughter, Hina-'a-ulu-ā. Naturally, as she grew to adulthood and he aged, he worried about the future of his kingdom. He urged his daughter to marry. "Choose from one of the chiefs who come here to court you," he said. Indeed, young chiefs came from all the islands, boasted of their accomplishments, recited their genealogies, and attempted to win the beautiful chiefess by performing all sorts of athletic and martial arts. They called her Ho'oipo-malanai (*Sweetheart of the Gentle Breeze*), and they showered her with gifts. Then, one day, there were eight chiefs from whom to choose, and Puna-'ai-koā-i'i was out of patience. "You must marry one of these chiefs," he said. "Which one?"

Hina-'a-ulu-ā shook her head. "All are equal," she said. "None is better than the other. I do not care. You choose."

Puna-'ai-koā-i'i sought a way out of his predicament. All of the

eight chiefs were proud men who could command a small army, if
need be, to avenge any insult. How to choose one of them so that all
remained contented? Puna-'ai-koā-i'i consulted with his high priest.
They thought of a plan that might well work. There would be a
contest. The eight chiefs were called before Puna-'ai-koā-i'i who
explained the rules. This was to be a contest of strength and speed.
A *lei palaoa* (whale tooth pendant on a necklace of woven human
hair) would be sent to the island of Ka'ula, a rocky islet off the southern coast of Ni'ihau. Each chief was to sail a canoe to Ka'ula with no
more than three other men to serve as paddlers. The first to retrieve
the *lei palaoa* and return would win the chiefess.

The eight chiefs were pleased; all could live with the result of
such a contest. It was truly the best man who would win. They all
prepared their canoes, and Puna-'ai-koā-i'i sent his *lei palaoa* to
Ka'ula, almost a hundred miles away from Wailua. When all was
ready, Puna-'ai-koā-i'i announced that the race would begin at dawn
the following morning. Throughout all the excitement, only Hina-
'a-ulu-ā remained indifferent.

During the late afternoon before the contest, almost at twilight,
a large voyaging canoe, painted red with red sails and a chief's pen-
nant flying from the mast, anchored off shore. The chief standing
on the broad *pola* (platform) between the hulls was dressed in full
regalia: *mahiole* (feather helmet), *'ahu'ula* (feather cloak), feather
malo (loincloth). He was tall, his hair was tinged with red, and
everyone speculated as to who he was. He was invited to join in the
evening festivities, and after a short time, Hina-'a-ulu-ā announced
to her father that she had chosen a husband.

It was too late, he informed her. Nothing could prevent the forth-
coming race for her hand. The newcomer, who said his name was
Mo'ikeha, had been attracted by the beautiful sweetheart of the gentle breeze. When the contest, its reason, its rules, its outcome were
explained to him, Mo'ikeha asked if he could enter the race. The
other contestants only wished to be assured that the stranger's genealogy was at least equal to theirs.

Mo'ikeha himself chanted his genealogy. "Nana'ulu the husband, Ulukou the wife," he began and continued down the generations. Then he chanted: "Kekupahaikala the husband, Maihikea
the wife; Maweke the husband, Naiolaukea the wife."

The crowd, who was listening intently, buzzed at this news.
Everyone knew Maweke was the leader of a voyaging canoe from

the south who had arrived two generations earlier. Already many of his family's stories were related by the storytellers.

Moʻikeha continued, "Muli-ʻele-aliʻi the father, Wehelani the mother; Moʻikeha the man, Hina-a-ʻulu-ā the wife!" The audience enjoyed the boast.

The eight chiefs admitted that Moʻikeha's genealogy was impeccable and were perfectly agreeable to his entering the race. None of them could see how the stranger could prepare himself overnight for such a trek. Indeed all that evening and far into the night, Moʻikeha and Hina-ʻa-ulu-ā talked and laughed until even she was afraid he could not possibly perform well in the morning's contest for her hand.

At dawn the contestants were ready at the beach. There were nine canoes, nine contestants, all eager to go except for one. Moʻikeha was telling Hina-ʻa-ulu-ā how glad he was to see her again. Puna-ʻai-koā-iʻi gave the signal to depart and eight contestants ran for their canoes, jumped in, paddled furiously to get through the breakers, hoisted their sails into the softly blowing breeze, and settled in for the hundred miles to Kaʻulu and the hundred miles back again. Moʻikeha loitered on the beach until Hina-ʻa-ulu-ā's anxiety sent him to his canoe. His was a small canoe, and he had only one helper on board instead of three. The helper had a huge covered calabash between his knees. The onlookers thought he was taking his fishing gear and commented that the added weight in the canoe would be of no help at all. Moʻikeha leisurely entered his canoe, picked up his paddle, and propelled the canoe through the breakers. Once at sea the two men stepped the mast and raised the sail. The onlookers gasped as the sail filled and ballooned as though a fierce wind storm had caught it. Within moments the canoe shot out of sight.

Unknown to everyone on shore, Moʻikeha's companion was Laʻa-maomao, owner of the large wooden calabash, which contained all the winds of the world. By opening the lid and uttering the wind's name, Laʻa-maomao could summon any wind he chose.

On the way to Kaʻula, one by one the other contestants were passed. Moʻikeha landed, claimed the prize, and was well on his way back to Wailua before the first of the eight reached the islet. The eight chiefs met together on Kaʻula. They agreed that the gods were obviously in favor of this stranger, and there was no cause for any of them to be angry. Furthermore, they would pledge themselves to his service. Thus the eight were as merry as any at the wedding festivities of Mo'ikeha and Hina-'a-ulu-ā.

Mo'ikeha's *kahuna nui*, Kama-hua-lele, as he had so often before and would often again, chanted the *mele inoa* (name chant) always associated with Mo'ikeha:

O Mo'ikeha, ka Lani nana e noho	O Mo'ikeha, the chief who is to reside,
Nohuku'u lani ia Hawai'i—a!	My chief will reside on Hawai'i—a!
Ola, ola, o kalana ola!	Life, life, o buoyant life!
Ola ke ali'i, ke kahuna,	Live shall the chief and priest,
Ola ke kilo, ke kauwa	Live shall the seer and the slave,
Noho ia Hawai'i a lu lana,	Dwell on Hawaii and be at rest,
A kani mo'opuna i Kaua'i.	And attain old age on Kaua'i.
O Kaua'i ka moku—a!	O Kaua'i is the island—a!
O Mo'ikeha ke ali'i.	O Mo'ikeha is the chief!

Mo'ikeha

Mo'ikeha was the grandson of Maweke who had come from Kahiki and settled on O'ahu. His father was Muli-'ele-ali'i, who had ruled over part of O'ahu. The oldest of his sons, Kumuhonua, inherited the O'ahu lands when Muli-'ele-ali'i died. Mo'ikeha joined his other brother 'Olopana and his sister Ha'inakolo when they moved to Waipi'o on Hawai'i.

Most important of all, Mo'ikeha took his adopted son, La'a, with him. La'a must have been hardly more than an infant at this time. He was a descendent of another famous traveler, Paumakua, who had settled on O'ahu at the same time as Maweke. La'a, to judge from his future activities, was trained from infancy in the knowledge of the ten levels of priesthood. How and why Mo'ikeha adopted La'a is not stated in any surviving legend, but obviously the *hānai* (foster) bond remained extremely strong.

'Olopana married Lu'ukia, daughter of Hikapoloa, a chief of Kohala, Hawai'i. They had two daughters.

Ha'inakolo married her cousin from Kahiki. The story of how her future husband wooed her, took her back to Tahiti and deserted her, her arrival back on Hawai'i island, her madness and recovery, as well as the saga of her son, Leimakani, form a complex of stories that well illustrates the ethos of the time.

After several years, Waipi'o was devastated by a hurricane. Leaving his daughters behind, 'Olopana and his followers sailed for Kahiki on five large canoes. Mo'ikeha and La'a went with him. They reached Ra'iātea in the Society Islands, and 'Olopana was given a district of land called Moa-'ula-nui-ākea (Red, Great, Widespread, Sacred Harbor). Mo'ikeha built his house near that of his brother, which he named Lanikeha (Heavenly Resting Place). La'a, as a priest, lived in a heiau on the slopes of Kapaahu, a tall mountain that dominated the district.

Mo'ikeha became famous for his hospitality, sparing nothing to make his life comfortable and entertaining. He refused to marry, saying that he already had a son in La'a. He did, however, fall in love with his brother's wife, Lu'ukia, and she with him. 'Olopana had no objections.

A local chief, Mua, also fell in love with Lu'ukia, but she would have nothing to do with him, which only increased his hidden rage. He began to drop hints in Lu'ukia's ears. From time to time Mo'ikeha would go to visit his foster son, La'a, and be gone overnight, but, Mua said, this was really so he could see another woman. Jealous, Lu'ukia wrapped herself with a cord in such a way that the ends of the cord were completely hidden. Mo'ikeha would never again be able to sleep with her.

Mua also dropped hints to 'Olopana, suggesting that Mo'ikeha's style of living was designed to make 'Olopana seem stingy, and that he was currying favor with other chiefs with the intention of overthrowing 'Olopana. 'Olopana publicly suggested that his brother might consider a more modest style of living, since that would better suit his position.

Mo'ikeha had never for a moment thought of betraying his brother or Lu'ukia. Humiliated and insulted, Mo'ikeha replied that he would leave Ra'iātea and return to Hawai'i. 'Olopana, now realizing that he had gone too far, tried to persuade Mo'ikeha to forget his rash words and stay. But Mo'ikeha had made up his mind.

Mo'ikeha readied his canoe on which he had sailed from Hawai'i. It was named Ka-ulua (The Jackfish). The canoe was almost a hundred feet long, and there was plenty of room for the forty people on board and their provisions. The navigator was Kama-hua-lele, a kilo-kilo (astrologer) who understood the stars and how to steer by them. He was also a poet and the kahu (guardian) of Mo'ikeha, as well as his kahuna nui. Also on board were Mo'ikeha's female relatives Makapu'u and Makaoa, and his male relatives Kumukahi and Hae-

hae. One of his priests was Moʻokini, another Laʻa-maomao, priest of the wind calabash, and the third was Holoholokū. There were also a host of men, navigators, sailing masters, his immediate attendants, and his favorites.

Laʻa, Moʻikeha's foster son, remained on Raʻiātea.

This was the man Hina-ʻa-ulu-ā welcomed to the shores of Wailua. He never again left the island.

After his marriage to Hina-ʻa-ulu-ā, the daughter of Puna-ʻai-koā-iʻi, Moʻikeha decided to build a *heiau* where his children would be born. Moʻikeha sent a messenger to Puna-ʻai-koā-iʻi with four *hinalea* fish, some taro and a shallow calabash of water. Puna-ʻai-koā-iʻi was curious and asked why the existing *heiau* Mele-aha-a-Nounou, which was situated atop Nounou ridge, wouldn't do.

It, the messenger replied, was considered by Moʻikeha to be useful only as a latrine, and that only when a *heiau* was built where Moʻikeha was then living would all be well.

The chief asked the messenger: "Couldn't you bring him here to me?"

The messenger answered: "He will not come until a house is built, a house that will take one day to build. Then you two will meet each other."

Immediately Puna-ʻai-koā-iʻi ordered all the people of Wailua to build a meeting house in one day. The two chiefs met there and discussed future plans. The new *heiau* was named Holoholokū after Moʻikeha's *kahuna*. Here, on the *pōhaku hānau* (birthing stones), Hina-ʻa-ulu-ā gave birth to her three sons, Hoʻokamaliʻi, Haulani-nui-ai-ākea, and Kila. From then on any *aliʻi nui* needed to be born in this place.

When his sons were grown, Moʻikeha wanted to see his foster son, Laʻa, again. He decided to send one of his sons to Raʻiātea to bring Laʻa to Wailua. He called the three together. "I intend to send one of you boys to find your brother Laʻa, and bring him back here so I can talk with him once more before I die," he told them.

The young men were enthusiastic. They all called out: "*Owau ke kiʻi!* Let me go!" over and over again. Very quickly evidence of ill-feeling among them became apparent.

Now Moʻikeha confronted the same problem that had faced Puna-ʻai-koā-iʻi: how to make a choice that would appease all contestants and not lead to bickering and hurt feelings or worse. Like his father-in-law, he thought of a contest. "I have decided to give you a test," he told his three sons. "The boy who shall excel over the others, he will be the one to go and bring your brother."

Each youngster was told to make a ti-leaf canoe. They would launch their canoes from one bank of the river, and they must sail to the other side where Moʻikeha would be waiting, sitting in the water with outstretched legs. Whoever owned the ti-leaf canoe that sailed between his thighs would be the one to sail south. "Under no condition are you to have a second trial," he said.

The day and hour of the contest came. Moʻikeha sat down at the edge of the river, his legs spread apart, facing the wind. The boys gathered on the opposite bank. Hoʻokamaliʻi set his canoe down in the water and aimed for the desired landing, but it missed the mark, sailing off in another direction. Then Haulani-nui-ai-ākea carefully placed his leaf canoe in the water, but it, too, missed its mark entirely. Kila launched his canoe, and it sailed directly to his father and passed between his thighs. Kila had won the cherished privilege to sail his father's canoe to Raʻiātea, thousands of miles to the south.

The two older brothers were very angry, and from then on they plotted to find some way to injure or kill Kila. Hina-ʻa-ulu-ā quickly became aware of this hatred and warned Kila never to be alone with his brothers on land or on sea.

Ka-ulua, Moʻikeha's voyaging canoe, was made ready. Sacrifices were offered, and the omens were favorable. Kama-hua-lele once again was the principle navigator. Holoholokū also came aboard with nine other men, and the canoe sailed south. Wind and weather remained favorable even though Kila stopped frequently, for he was following in reverse his father's footsteps and there were many who remembered Moʻikeha. At each stop, storytellers delighted in recounting the following exchange:

KILA:	*Welina hoi ia oe.*	My greetings to you.
KAMAʻĀINA:	*Owai oe?*	Who are you?
KILA:	*O Kila i uka,*	I am Kila of the uplands,
	O Kila i kai,	Kila of the lowlands,
	O Kila pa wahine,	I am Kila, the last child
	A Hina-ʻa-ulu-ā	of Hina-ʻa-ulu-ā
	O kama au a Moʻikeha.	the offspring of Moʻikeha.
KAMAʻĀINA:	*Ke ola la no ka o Moʻikeha?*	Is Moʻikeha then still living?
KILA:	*Ke ola la no.*	He is still living.

KAMAʻĀINA: *Ka walea ana?*   What is he doing?

KILA: *I walea ia Kauai i ka la hiki*   He is indulging in ease on Kauai
ae a po iho, i keekee a ka nalu   where the sun rises and sets;
o Makaiwa, i ke kahuli mai a   where the surf of Makaiwa curves
ka pua kukui o Puna, o ka   and bends; where the kukui blos-
waihalau o Wailua, noho no   soms of Puna change; where the
ia Kauai a make ia Kauai.   waters of Wailua stretch out. He
    will live and die on Kauai.

When Kila reached Moa-ʻula-nui-ākea on Raʻiātea, Mua came to the beach to greet Kila. Years before, Mua, jealous of Moʻikeha, had poisoned the affections of both ʻOlopana and Luʻukia. When his brother and his lover had believed this slander, Moʻikeha had left the island, insulted and humiliated. Even then Mua had not been able to win Luʻukia's affection.

Reminded of this story by either Kama-hua-lele or Holoholokū, Kila seized Mua and tied him hand and foot. Mua was placed in the depths of the hold on one side of the canoe, and Kila and all his men urinated on him until, after three days, he drowned. Moʻikeha had been revenged.

When he stepped ashore, storytellers related: "At the sight of Kila, the crowd began to shout, admiring his beauty. Even the ants were heard to sing his praise; the birds sang, the pebbles rumbled, the shells cried out, the grass withered, the smoke hung low, the rain-bow appeared, the thunder was heard, the dead came to life, the hairless dogs were seen and countless spirits of all kinds were seen." All elements of nature recognized the presence of a true hero, as is often told in legends.

Then Kila greeted his uncle ʻOlopana and his aunt Luʻukia. Asked about Moʻikeha, Kila replied in a chant:

I walea ia Kauai,   He is indulging in ease on Kauaʻi,
I ka la hiki ae a po iho,   Where the sun shines and sets again,
I ke kee a ka nalu o Makaiwa,   Where the surf of Makaiwa curves
    and bends,

I ka hiki mai a ka la maluna,   Where the sun comes up over,
O ke kalukalu o Kewā,   The kalukalu of Kewā,
O ka wai halau o Wailua.   The cool and calm shade of Wailua.

O ka lealea o ka mai o kuu makuahine,	And the entrancing favors of my mother,
O Hina-'a-ulu-ā, ho'oipo-malanai.	O Hina-'a-ulu-ā, sweetheart of the gentle breeze.
O kahi noho no o Kauai a make.	He will live and die on Kaua'i.

Kila found La'a at Kapaahu. He gave La'a a feather cape of brilliant yellow feathers, a present from Mo'ikeha, and told him his *makua hānai* (foster father) desired to see him once again before he died. La'a accepted the invitation, and in a short time, La'a, in his own canoe, joined Kila for the long voyage to Hawai'i.

La'a-mai-Kahiki

When La'a's canoe slid onto the sands of 'Aliō beach at Wailua, father and son greeted each other warmly. La'a had announced his arrival with the beating of a huge drum made of a hollowed out coconut trunk covered on its open end by shark skin, the first of its kind seen in Hawai'i. It had a deep voice and from then on was beaten to announced the birth of chiefs on the birthing stones at Holoholokū *heiau,* where the drum was kept until the ancient religion was destroyed in 1819.

La'a also carried with him two sets of ideas that transformed the existing society.

First, La'a brought a new god to join Kū and Kāne. This was Lono-i-ka-'ou-ali'i *(Lono-in-the-chiefly-signs-in-the-heavens).* Lono was the god of agriculture, medicine, and of harvest festivities. The rituals connected with Lono were milder than those of Kū, since no humans were ever sacrificed on an altar dedicated to Lono. The Lono temple was of the *māpele* type. This meant that *lama* wood was used to construct all the buildings within the *heiau* walls since *lama* also means "enlightenment." The buildings were thatched with leaves of *ti.* The purpose of a *māpele* was to have a place to ask Lono's help in all agricultural pursuits, including requests for life-giving rain.

When a *māpele* had been constructed at Wailua, La'a carried an idol of Lono from his canoe to the *heiau.* This is the first known idol on Kaua'i. With the image came priests who introduced new rules, rites, and customs, more rigid than the Kāne or Kū ceremonies. The Lono *heiau* were now closed to the people, and they no longer participated in the ceremonies.

Second, La'a also established the first *kumukānāwai*, an edict or law. These edicts were often designed to safeguard the rank and position of an *ali'i*, but sometimes, inadvertently, these *kapu* had the effect of safeguarding the rights of commoners. From the time of La'a, every ruling chief issued his own law, which was named and could be inherited by the next generation. Each of these laws also carried a penalty, frequently death, for anyone who dared break them. La'a's *kumukānāwai* were the *kapu lama* (torch edict) and the *kapu loulu* (loulu palm commandment). One of these was named Ua-ala-ka-wai, but exactly what this law said or the punishment associated with it is no longer known.

The existing legends are silent concerning La'a's stay on Kaua'i. We do not know what he did, or what he and his foster father talked about, or how long he stayed. Before he left Kaua'i, La'a, by then known as La'a-mai-Kahiki (*Sacredness from Kahiki*), promised Mo'i-keha that he would return to carry Mo'ikeha's bones to Ra'iātea and bury them at Lanikeha, Mo'ikeha's former home on the slopes of Kapaahu.

In memory of La'a's stay on Kaua'i and in thanks for the bounty that La'a's god Lono-i-ka-'ou-ali'i brought, an annual custom developed. A basket shaped like a canoe was made from sticks of peeled *wauke*. This was called *wa'a au ahu* (swimming altar canoe) and represented the canoe in which La'a returned to Ra'iātea. The basket, like La'a's canoe, was filled with all sorts of food. It was then tied between the crossbeams of an outrigger canoe that was paddled out to sea. Here the *wa'a au ahu* was cut free and allowed to drift away, disappearing over the horizon just as La'a's canoe had done.

La'a reached Kualoa on the north coast of O'ahu where he was persuaded to remain for a time. A large house was built for him, and he was liberally supplied with food and all other necessities that make up a household, the finest that could be found.

The priests knew that La'a was a direct descendant of Paumakua, a voyager who had settled on O'ahu three generations earlier, and that this line was in danger of dying out. The priests pleaded with La'a to marry and sire a child, saying that he would be free to leave once the bride was pregnant. La'a agreed. Elated, the priests began to search for a suitable bride. She must have an impeccable genealogy, have a *kapu* of her own that she could leave her child, and in general fulfill the tangible signs of *ali'i* rank. In addition, the choice of any one chiefess should not stir up anger, jealousy, and perhaps warfare in a family whose daughter was not chosen. It was a delicate business.

Before long, however, the priests had narrowed their choice to three. They asked Laʻa to make the final decision, since that way any animosities from the other families could be dealt with. Laʻa refused. Whether he married and had a child was a matter for the priests; it did not matter to him.

The priests finally hit upon a solution that satisfied everyone. Laʻa would marry all three chiefesses: Hoaka-nui, the daughter of Lono-ka-ʻehu of Kualoa; Waolena, daughter of a chief from Ka-ʻalaea; and Mano, daughter of a Kāneʻohe chief. All three were beautiful, Laʻa was handsome, and their wedding was celebrated with great enthusiasm.

Many months later, the three wives of Laʻa each gave birth to a son on the same day. This "triple canoe" is remembered by this chant:

O Ahukini, O Laʻa—a— O Laʻa—a—	O Ahukini, O Laʻa—a— O Laʻa —a—
O Laʻamaikahiki ke aliʻi,	O Laʻa from Kahiki, the chief,
O Ahukini-a-Laʻa,	O Ahukini-a-Laʻa,
O Kūkona-a-Laʻa	O Kūkona-a-Laʻa,
O Lauli-a-Laʻa, mākua,	O Lauli-a-Laʻa, the father,
O nā pūkolu a Laʻa-mai-Kahiki,	The triple canoe of Laʻa-mai-Kahiki,
He mau hiapo kapu a Laʻa,	The sacred firstborn (children) of Laʻa,
Hoʻokahi no ka lā i hānau ai.	Who were born on the same day.

Lauli-a-Laʻa was the last to be born. His mother, as soon as she heard that the other wives had given birth, began to slap her abdomen to induce labor, which was successful. Ever since, she has been known as Mano-opu-paʻipaʻi (Mano Who Slapped Her Abdomen).

All three left descendants, and the line of Paumakua, the voyager from the south, never died out, thanks to Laʻa-mai-Kahiki.

After a year at Kualoa, Laʻa once again prepared his canoe and sailed home to Raʻiātea.

During the following centuries, Laʻa was revered as a god in the

Society Islands, Rarotonga, and among the Maoris of New Zealand. As a god he had the attributes of greatness and glory. These qualities he gave to the gatherings of the other gods at any human ceremony enacted in this mortal realm.

La'a was not always gentle and kind. When provoked, his temper flared and remained strong for a long time. He then would call up a strong wind named Rapati'a (*Steady blowing*), which caused great destruction. La'a's anger could only be appeased after Rapati'a had claimed land, not hard to do on low-lying coral atolls.

La'a's Ra'iātea wife was Tu-papa (*Rock Abider*) and their son Te-va-humuhumu (*Soothing Wind*) also became a god. He healed wounds and infections inflicted on the battlefield.

After the departure of La'a from Kaua'i, Mo'ikeha arranged for the future of his sons with Hina-'a-ulu-ā. Ho'okamali'i, the oldest, moved to O'ahu to become the ruling chief of the Kona district and settled on the plains of 'Ewa. Kila went to Waipi'o on Hawai'i. Even though Mo'ikeha and his brother 'Olopana had left these lands, they never abandoned their claim to this valley. Haulani-nui-ai-ākea remained on Kaua'i, where on Mo'ikeha's death, he became *ali'i nui*.

Mo'ikeha's bones were hidden somewhere in Hā'ena on the north shore while Kila sailed south to Ra'iātea to bring the news to La'a-mai-Kahiki. It was time to fulfill his promise. La'a-mai-Kahiki collected the bones of his foster father and immediately returned home.

Haulani-nui-ai-ākea

Haulani-nui-ai-ākea proved to be an unsatisfactory *ali'i nui*. Other Kaua'i chiefs, under the leadership of Ke-oloewa-a-Kamaua, deposed their unfit ruler. Ke-oloewa-a-Kamaua was a Moloka'i chief married to one of Maweke's granddaughters, thus keeping this affair in the family.

Haulani-nui-ai-ākea was easily overthrown. When Ke-oloewa-a-Kamaua refused the throne, Kila was asked to come to Kaua'i and take over as *ali'i nui*. He came but found his heart was not on Kaua'i. He placed the highest ranking *ali'i* in the family, the beautiful Ka-'ili-lau-o-ke-koa, as paramount chief, returned to his canoe and sailed to Ra'iātea to remain for the rest of his life with his brother La'a-mai-Kahiki.

Ka-ʻili-lau-o-ke-koa

Ka-ʻili-lau-o-ke-koa was very beautiful with cheeks glowing like the rising sun. Her genealogy has not survived, and we do not know if she is the daughter of Laʻa or, perhaps, Haulani-nui-ai-ākea. She is frequently referred to as the granddaughter of Moʻikeha and Hina-ʻa-ulu-ā. Her *kahu* (personal guardian and attendant) was Lehua-wehe, the daughter of the sorceress Waha. Waha also had another daughter, Ka-hale-lehua, the goddess of rain, and a son, Ka-ua-kahi-aliʻi.

Ka-ʻili-lau-o-ke-koa was an expert *kōnane* player (a game similar to checkers) and a champion rider of surfboards at Makaīwa near the mouth of the Wailua river. Naturally there were many men who desired to marry her, including Ke-liʻi-koa, high chief of the Kona chiefdom. She ignored them all.

Her advisors, realizing the benefits of joining the Puna and Kona chiefdoms peacefully, betrothed her to Ke-liʻi-koa. Invitations to the wedding were sent out, and when Waha received hers, she muttered, "The right will prevail."

Her son, Ka-ua-kahi-aliʻi, thus heard of the beautiful chiefess and decided he wanted to marry her himself. He took up his nose flute, Kanikawi. This was a cylinder of bamboo with holes drilled in it. When blown into through the nose, a melody of five notes could be produced, and Kanikawi's value was that it was very loud and could be heard a long distance. From his home at Pihana-ka-lani in the uplands of Wailua, Ka-ua-kahi-aliʻi sent a melodic message to his beloved on the night breeze.

E piʻi ka nahele,	Climb into the upland forest
E ike ia Ka-wai-kini,	And greet Ka-wai-kini,
Nana ia Pihana-ka-lani,	Look down at Pihana-ka-lani,
I keia manu hulu maʻemaʻe,	Where the beautiful bird feathers
Nono pu me Ka-hale-lehua,	Are as sun-red as Ka-hale-lehua,
Punahele ia Ka-ua-kahi-aliʻi.	Beloved sister of Ka-ua-kahi-aliʻi.
E Kaili, e Kaili, e!	Oh, Kaili, Kaili!
E Kaili, e Kaili, e!	Oh, Kaili, Kaili!
E Ka-ʻili-lau-o-ke-koa,	Ka-ʻili-lau-o-ke-koa,
E Ka-ʻili-lau-o-ke-koa,	Ka-ʻili-lau-o-ke-koa,
Moʻopuna a Hoʻoipo-i-ka-malanai,	Granddaughter of Hoʻoipo-i-ka-malanai,

Hiwahiwa a ka Lehua-wehe!	The darling of Lehua-wehe!
Aia ka nani i Wai-ehu,	There is the beauty at Wai-ehu,
I ka wai kaili puuwai o ka makemake.	In the stream that overflows my heart with desire.
Makemake au i ke kalukalu o Kewā,	I desire to rest in the soft rushes of Kewā,
E heʻe ana i ka nalu o Maka-iwa.	And to surf in the waves of Maka-iwa.
He iwaiwa oe na ke aloha,	You are a wild fern calmed by love
I Wailua nui hōano.	At Wailua-nui-hōano.
Anoano ka hale, aohe kanaka,	Uninhabited is the house, there are no people,
Ua laʻoe no ke one o Ali-ō.	You are content on the sands of ʻAliō.
Aia ka ipo i ka nahele.	Here is your lover in the upland forest!

Intrigued, Ka-ʻili-lau-o-ke-koa decided to follow the sound, and after getting her guards drunk with *ʻawa* and fermented sweet potato, she and her *kahu* began to climb Kuamoʻo-loa-a-Kāne ridge, which leads from the river mouth to Wailua-uka. Ka-hale-lehua, who eventually became the goddess of Kauaʻi rain, sent a heavy mist and blinding rain to test Ka-ʻili-lau-o-ke-koa. Ka-ʻili-lau-o-ke-koa was stubborn and took shelter in the hollow of an old tree. When the rain stopped, she kept on, overcoming other obstacles sent by Waha. At dawn, Ka-ʻili-lau-o-ke-koa reached Pihana-ka-lani and was greeted by Ka-hale-lehua and given dry clothes. After a meal, Ka-ʻili-lau-o-ke-koa searched for Ka-ua-kahi-aliʻi and found him. She, enthralled by the handsome stranger, remained with him.

After a few days, her guardians and advisors became alarmed and searched for their chiefess. Ka-hale-lehua sent the fine rains, the shower reaching to the sky, and heavy rains to hide and protect the lovers. In spite of the resulting floods, they were found. Ka-ʻili-lau-o-ke-koa was carried in the arms of her attendants, as favorites were, but Ka-ua-kahi-aliʻi had his hands tied behind his back with ropes. They were brought back to Wailua-nui-hōano. Ka-ua-kahi-aliʻi was treated as a prisoner and tied to the center post of a prison. Two days later, a boy named Ke-kalukalu-o-Kewā passed by and asked Ka-ua-kahi-aliʻi if he had been given any food or water. When Ka-ua-kahi-aliʻi said he had not, the boy brought him water in one covered coconut shell bowl and food in another. Crawling in under the thatch so the guards would not see him, Ke-kalukalu-o-Kewā fed Ka-ua-kahi-aliʻi over the next few days.

Meanwhile Ka-ʻili-lau-o-ke-koa told her father of her adventures and of her desire to be the wife of Ka-ua-kahi-aliʻi. At last he agreed that she could, provided he could give his genealogy proving he was an *aliʻi*. Surprised at his vigor after what they thought were four or five days of fasting, they listened intently as Ka-ua-kahi-aliʻi chanted his family lineage, which proved to be high indeed. Thus Ka-ua-kahi-aliʻi, with the aid of his nose flute won the beautiful girl.

Kekalukalu-o-Kewā, for his kind deed, became Ka-ua-kahi-aliʻi's great friend and in time became the *konohiki* of the Wailua ahupuaʻa.

Ke-liʻi-koa, angry at losing Ka-ʻili-lau-o-ke-koa, while surfing in his canoe tried to run over Ka-ua-kahi-aliʻi who was on his surfboard. Instead, it was he who was wounded, and he returned home, leaving his *kālaimoku* (counselor) Piʻi-o-Kalalau at Wailua with instructions to kill Ka-ua-kahi-aliʻi as soon as possible. Piʻi-o-Kalalau befriended Ka-ua-kahi-aliʻi and invited him to his house. As Ka-ua-kahi-aliʻi stooped to enter, a heavy log fell on him and broke his shoulder. Piʻi-o-Kalalau then attacked him with his spear. Ka-ʻili-lau-o-ke-koa had been suspicious of Piʻi-o-Kalalau and had followed them. Seeing Piʻi-o-Kalalau attack her husband, she threw a rock, which stunned Piʻi-o-Kalalau long enough for Ka-ua-kahi-aliʻi to escape. Then Ka-ʻili-lau-o-ke-koa gathered her warriors to dispose of Piʻi-o-Kalalau, but he fought back and, being a large, strong man, managed to escape. This was the first battle in what was to be several centuries of war between Kona and Puna.

After the marriage celebration, Ka-ua-kahi-aliʻi and Ka-ʻili-lau-o-ke-koa decided to travel to all the other islands. One reason was that Ka-ua-kahi-aliʻi wanted to see if there was any other woman in Hawaiʻi who could compare with Ka-ʻili-lau-o-ke-koa's beauty. On Hawaiʻi, he met Lāʻie-i-ka-wai and found that she was almost as beautiful as Ka-ʻili-lau-o-ke-koa.

When they returned to Wailua, the local high chiefs, the low chiefs, and the country *aliʻi* gathered to hear their news. Among these was ʻAi-wohi-kupuna. Their description of Lāʻie-i-ka-wai inflamed ʻAi-wohi-kupuna, and he desired to see her for himself. He took his five sisters with him and tried to woo Lāʻie-i-ka-wai. The sisters failed to win Lāʻie-i-ka-wai for him, and ʻAi-wohi-kupuna abandoned them. They soon became honored *kahu* (attendants) of Lāʻie-i-ka-wai.

When Ka-ua-kahi-aliʻi died only a few years after his marriage, Ke-liʻi-koa gathered his army to invade Wailua, capture Ka-ʻili-lau-o-ke-koa, marry her, and join the two kingdoms. Ka-ʻili-lau-o-ke-koa, as requested by Ka-ua-kahi-aliʻi, had married their friend Ke-kalukalu-o-Kewā. The royal couple waited for Ke-liʻi-koa at the top of Kuamoʻo ridge. Here the two armies fought from early morning until noon. Ke-liʻi-koa's attack was so fierce that the Puna troops slowly began to fall back. Finally the Puna men took shelter behind a stone wall, many of them seriously wounded, hard pressed by the Kona warriors. At a particularly bleak moment, Ka-ʻili-lau-o-ke-koa appeared with new help. She had organized and armed every woman in Wailua, and they rushed on the battlefield eager to help their men. Suddenly Ke-liʻi-koa's forces were on the defensive. Ke-liʻi-koa challenged Ke-kalukalu-o-Kewā to single combat. He did not hesitate. The two men fought but, tired as he was, Ke-kalukalu-o-Kewā could not avoid two quick thrusts of Ke-liʻi-koa's spear and sank to the ground. Ke-liʻi-koa raised his spear to finish the fallen chief, but Ka-ʻili-lau-o-ke-koa flung her *pīkoi* (tripping club) at him. Her aim was true. The three cords of the *pīkoi* twisted around Ke-liʻi-koa's upraised arm and head. One of the stones on the end of the cord struck him in the temple, and he fell dead. Then the Kona army was decimated, and the body of their chief was taken to a *heiau* and sacrificed to the gods.

When Ka-ʻili-lau-o-ke-koa died, she was childless. There was no direct heir to the chiefdom. Haulani-nui-ai-ākea, the oldest son of Moʻikeha, had settled on Oʻahu; the second son, Hāʻula-nui-ai-ākea, had been deposed; Kila, Moʻikeha's third son, was in Raʻiātea. The chiefdom of Puna on Kauaʻi was offered to the oldest of Laʻa-mai-Kahiki's three sons.

Ahukini-a-Laʻa accepted.

3

WĀ PŌPILIKIA
Troubled Times

WHEN AHUKINI-A-LAʻA ARRIVED ON KAUAʻI, HE FOUND THAT the Puna kingdom was already at war with Kona, a legacy of his cousin Ka-ʻili-lau-o-ke-koa. There was no longer enough room on the island for two aggressive kingdoms and the dream of uniting them burned brightly for a hundred years. This was a century of great heroes. The deeds of Palila, Ka-uʻi-lani, Kama-puaʻa, and Limaloa were shaped into heroic sagas that became the delight of storytellers and their audiences.

Ahukini-a-Laʻa

The *kumukānāwai* (sacred edict) of Ahukini-a-Laʻa was named Puʻua, a word that today is translated as "being choked, suffocated, or strangled, as in swallowing food." What the law stated and the punishment for breaking it remain forever unknown.

Ahukini-a-Laʻa married Haʻi-a-Kamaʻiʻo, granddaughter of Lua-ʻehu, one of the southern emigrant chiefs who was a contemporary of Laʻa-mai-Kahiki. Her family was said by some to be descended from A-kalana, the father of the famous Polynesian trickster, Māui-kiʻikiʻi. Perhaps as a tribute to their new *aliʻi nui wahine*, many of Māui-kiʻikiʻi's exploits were now retold as though they had occurred on Kauaʻi.

Māui-ki'iki'i, the storytellers said, lived at Wailua-nui-hōano. His mother, who lived just above 'Ōpae-ka'a waterfall, once sighed for cooked food, since at that time no one knew the secret of making fire. Hina told her son that the mudhens ('alae) knew how to make fire, since she had often seen their fires on the plains below at Papa-'ena'ena (Burning hot plain). The mudhens were very cautious and only lit their fires when Māui-ki'iki'i and his brothers were in their canoe at the deep-sea fishing grounds. Clever Māui-ki'iki'i replaced himself in the canoe with a carved image so that the mudhens thought he was on board. He dug a hole near the firepit of the wily birds and hid himself there. When the birds lit a fire, Māui-ki'iki'i caught the chief 'alae and demanded the secret of fire. The bird suggested a method, thinking that Māui-ki'iki'i would let her go to try it out, but Māui-ki'iki'i never let go of the bird through many impossible suggestions. At last Māui-ki'iki'i began to wring the bird's neck and the mudhen finally told the secret, that of rubbing a hardwood stick against a soft wood until the fire came. Māui-ki'iki'i got a fire going and burned the top of the 'alae's head, a red mark the birds carry to this day. His mother, Hina, finally ate hot cooked food prepared by her clever son.

Māui-ki'iki'i also wanted to catch the huge ulua (jackfish) named Lua'ehu, who was also the grandfather of Ha'i-a-Kama'i'o, according to certain storytellers who freely mixed elements from different legends. This fish was so huge that it was thought that islands were merely the humps of the fish's back. Māui-ki'iki'i wanted to draw all the islands of Hawai'i into one large landmass. Lua'ehu was warned of this by the 'alae birds on the plain of Wailua. Nonetheless Māui-ki'iki'i finally caught Lua'ehu and would have succeeded in drawing the islands of Kaua'i and O'ahu together except that he had taken into his canoe a gourd bailer that had floated by. When the bailer turned into a beautiful woman, the people on shore cried out at the sight of her. Māui-ki'iki'i's brothers, in spite of having been warned not to, turned to look, and Lua'ehu escaped the hook.

No legend has come down to us concerning any particular events during Ahukini-a-La'a's reign, only that he and Ha'i-a-Kama'i'o had a son, Kama-hano.

Kama-hano

Kama-hano lived with Ka-'auea-o-ka-lani, but nothing is known of her background. They had a son, Lu'anu'u.

It was at this time that the first warrior-hero of Kauaʻi appeared. The war between Kona and Puna flared up. Akua-pehu-ʻale of Kona swept ashore at Wailua and the surprised Puna chiefs fled for the uplands. Akua-pehu-ʻale was considered a *kupua*, a supernatural being who could take two forms, in this case, that of a man and that of a giant sea monster. He was greatly feared and hated even by the men on his side. Once he had vanquished the Puna forces, Akua-pehu-ʻale settled at the seashore.

One of the exiled chiefs, Ke-ʻāhua, found refuge in a remote valley in the Wailua uplands, which today bears his wife's name, Ka-uhao, daughter of Hono-uliuli and Ka-pā-lama of Oʻahu. Their first child was Lepe-a-moa, a *kupua*, who could take the form of a beautiful woman or a resplendently feathered chicken. She was taken at birth to be raised by her Oʻahu grandparents.

Shortly after their defeat, Ka-uhao gave birth to a son. That he was to become a great man was noted by the gods, for a great storm raged during his birth. Rain poured down and flooded the streams and rivers. Thunder roared, lightning flashed, earthquakes shook the earth, and a rainbow formed over his birthplace. It is no wonder that he was named Ka-uʻi-lani (*The Divine Athlete*).

He was taken by his father's parents, Lau-ka-ʻieʻie and Kani-a-ula, who bathed him daily in a spring called Wai-uʻi (*Water of Strength*), which conferred on him great strength and remarkable handsomeness. He grew up knowing he was in exile from his proper home in Wailua.

One day Ka-uʻi-lani approached his father. "If you follow my plan," he said, "we may be able to kill Akua-pehe-ʻale." Ke-ʻāhua listened and agreed to the plan. He sent workers into the mountains to cut down *ʻahakea* trees and shape them into spears. These were then carried to the foot of a precipice near the exile's home and set into the ground, sharp points facing the sky. Other places were also selected, and soon the area bristled with sharp *ʻahakea* spears.

During the night, Ka-uʻi-lani prayed to all the gods for their help. In the morning, the storytellers say, all the *ʻahakea* stakes had sprouted and their branches had interwoven into an impenetrable fence. That was the project for the first day.

The following morning, women collected *wauke* bark and pounded it into sheets of *kapa*. The men built two houses side by side according to Ka-uʻi-lani's specifications. Once again Ka-uʻi-lani prayed to all the gods and they came to help. All through the night there was the sound of axes ringing, trees falling, chisels carving and sculpting the wood. By dawn, the two houses were filled with carved wooden images dressed in fresh tapa. This was the work of the second day.

Then Ka-u'i-lani announced that all his preparations were ready. He ordered all the wood chips that had accumulated during the night burned in a huge bonfire. Akua-pehu-'ale saw the smoke from the fire and rushed to the spot. He found Ka-u'i-lani standing at the doorway of one of the two houses with a huge image on either side of him. Akua-pehu-'ale immediately prepared to fight the youth, but Ka-u'i-lani ordered, as warriors in those days could do, "Return to your place today. Tomorrow I shall come to you and battle you."

Akua-pehu-'ale hesitated. "Sweet is the fatness of this place," he said. "Your bones are soft and your skin still shines with youth. No, today is the day you will die."

Ka-u'i-lani replied, "This is my place. If I battle you and win, the pieces of your body will be mine to sacrifice and all your conquered land will be mine. Maybe you should die, for you are very old. Your eyelids droop, your skin is dry and hangs on you. This is not the day for us to fight. Go back to the beach and get ready. I will come down tomorrow."

Akua-pehu-'ale thought for a moment. The word of a warrior chief was sacred; if he promised to come tomorrow, he would come. Besides, the *kupua* reasoned, he could then pick a battlefield that would be more to his advantage. He went back to the beach.

Ka-u'i-lani told his father that during the fight to come he and his warriors were, first, to keep themselves protected by the growth of *'ahakea* and, second, to keep turning Akua-pehu-'ale toward the houses filled with the wooden images.

As promised at dawn of the appointed day, Ka-u'i-lani strode to the beach where the *kupua* awaited him. The two fought, and the sand of the battlefield rose in great clouds from their shifting feet. The warrior struck the *kupua* in the roof of his mouth with his spear and fell back to where the *'ahakea* spears waited. Blinded with anger and pain, Akua-pehu-'ale rushed onto the stakes, which wounded him even more. Ka-'āhua and his men forced the *kupua* to move toward the image-filled houses.

Once Akua-pehu-'ale arrived at the houses, the images themselves came to life. Even though Akua-pehu-'ale tore some of these images apart with his teeth, he grew very tired. Ka-u'i-lani jumped to one side, plunged his spear into the monster's side, and the *kupua* fell dead. Ka-u'i-lani rolled the body into one of the houses and offered a chant of worship and of sacrifice to the gods, thanking them for all the help they had given him. Then he set fire to the houses and burned the body of Akua-pehu-'ale and all the wooden images.

After a victor's feast, Ka-u'i-lani led his people back down to the river mouth of Wailua-nui-hōano and reinstated his father to his rightful place. Later Ka-u'i-lani sailed for O'ahu to find his sister, Lepe-a-moa, whom he had never seen.

Puna's war with Kona was not over yet, however. Kama-hano's son Lu'anu'u in his turn also faced a strong enemy.

Lu'anu'u

It is said that Lu'anu'u was a good chief and he made Kaua'i a productive farm. His government was considered a proper one and he was greatly admired in spite of the continuing war against the Kona kingdom. His consort was Ka-lani-moe-i-ka-wai-kai-'eli-ali'i, of whom nothing more than her name is known.

Lu'anu'u apparently was named after the grandfather of Ki'i, father of 'Ulu and Nana'ulu, a reminder that the ancient genealogies were told and stories remembered, and that Lu'anu'u's genealogy proved he was descended from the first man created in the ancient night by the gods.

When Ka-'auea-o-ka-lani, Lu'anu'u's mother, was living on O'ahu, she realized she was about to give birth and returned to Kaua'i. As the double canoe neared the shore, her birth pangs began and she sat on the edge of the *pola* (platform). There she gave birth and the infant plunged into the ocean. He was immediately rescued and placed in the *'anu'u* (tower) within Pōhaku-ha'ule *heiau*. Therefore, it has been claimed, his name was really Lu'u-nu'u, *lu'u* because he had fallen into the water and *nu'u* because he had been placed in the tower.

All references to Lu'anu'u indicate a close relationship to the Kona kingdom. Later, storytellers said he had been born at Pe'e-Kaua'i (*Hidden Kaua'i*) on the plains of Waimea just *makai* of Pali-uli, the land that Ola's Menehune ditch had made fertile. Lu'anu'u, they said, was raised at Māha'iha'i, the small flat area on the east bank of the Waimea river. His afterbirth was deposited at Luhi, the nearby beach where the *ali'i* lived. His placenta was hidden at Pe'ape'a-makawalu, a peak leading from Luhi to Ka-wai-kini, and his navel cord was given to the guardian rock at Kolo in Mānā.

These references to Lu'anu'u and the lands of Kona seem unlikely. They more likely were a way to assert a legitimate claim to Kona after it was defeated by Lu'anu'u's son, Kūkona.

The great warrior of Lu'anu'u's time was named Palila, the son of Ka-lua-o-pālena and Maihi-iki. He was taken from his mother at birth and raised by his grandmother Hina in the sacred temple of Alana-pō where he was trained in all the martial arts warriors of those days needed to know. He ate nothing but bananas, and there were two banana patches consecrated for his use, one along the banks of the Wailua, the other on the slopes of the Makaleha mountain range.

Palila, of course, learned all his martial arts well, and happily demonstrated his skills to his grandmother. Hina said, "Yes, you are halfway through your learning."

Palila and his teachers were astounded. What more did he have to learn?

Hina replied, "You use only your right arm. Now learn to use your left arm."

So Palila started over again until he could shift his dagger, war club or spear with blinding speed from one hand to the other, thus bewildering an enemy so that he was easily overcome.

On the day he finished this training, he heard the noise of battle echoing over the ridge that divided the plains of Puna from the plains of Koloa. He wanted to ask Hina what the noise meant, but she was gone from her usual place. Indeed she had gone to the battlefield on the Koloa plains to warn Ka-lua-o-pālena that his son Palila would be coming to help him. At that time, the outcome of many battles could be decided by one fight between two warriors.

Hina said to Ka-lua-o-pālena, "Be on your guard. Three warriors will come before you today. The first will be Ka-kohu-koko from Moloa'a. He claims it takes forty men to carry his war club. Do not choose him. The second will be Lupe-a-ka-wai-o-Wainiha. He will claim it takes 120 men to carry his war club. Do not choose him. Then will come a third warrior, twirling his war club in his right hand, then in his left hand. He will be the warrior by whose help you will conquer all of Kaua'i."

When Ka-kohu-koko appeared, he made his boast and twirled his war club threateningly. Ka-lua-o-pālena did not choose him and he returned in shame to Moloaʻa. Exactly the same thing happened to Lupe-a-ka-wai-o-Wainiha and he, too, left the battlefield and went home. But Palila did not present himself and, surprised and discouraged that Hina's words to him were not fulfilled, Ka-lua-o-pālena drew up his army in formation and prepared for a general battle.

Meanwhile, Palila followed the shouts and noises of impending battle, crossed the ridge, and stopped to look down on the dusty plains of Koloa, Weliweli and Pāʻā. He saw two armies facing each other. One was led by his father, Ka-lua-o-pālena, the other by the Kona chief Ka-maka-o-ka-lani. Palila stood on a high point now called Ke-komo-o-ke-anu (*Coming of the Cold*), where he was seen by the soldiers of both armies. It was obvious that the man standing in open view on the heights in his feathered helmet and cape, with a huge, shark-lined war club over his shoulder, was a formidable opponent, and cold fear gripped every soldier as they wondered if they would have to face such an enemy.

Palila saw that his father's army was drawn up on the open plain in the usual war formation, ready for face-to-face, hand-to-hand combat. Against him stood a thin formation of Kona soldiers. Palila realized that Ka-maka-o-ka-lani had hidden much of his force in a forest of ʻōhiʻa hā and *lehua* trees on one flank of the Puna army, obviously intending to have this hidden force drive down on Ka-lua-o-pālena and hoping to win the battle by surprise. Palila was outraged at such treachery. He went to the edge of the forest and with a blow of his war club knocked down a tree. It fell against its neighbor, uprooting it so that it fell against the tree beside it. In a short time, the entire forest had been felled in this manner. Most of Ka-maka-o-ka-lani's hidden army was killed.

Palila strode onto the battlefield and challenged the Kona chief to single combat. Ka-maka-o-ka-lani concentrated on the war club in Palila's right hand and did not notice the dagger in his left hand until too late. Once Ka-maka-o-ka-lani died, the rest of the Kona forces broke and ran.

Ka-lua-o-pālena approached his son and stretched out on the ground before him. Palila raised his war club over his father's head. The Puna warriors, fearing the worst, fell on their stomachs in fear, not daring to look up.

Not knowing quite what to do, for he did not fully understand why his father was offering himself as a sacrifice, if indeed that was what he was doing, Palila lowered his war club, rested its end on the ground, and leaned on it. It sank into the ground and when Palila pulled it up, a steady spring of water followed it.

Hina crossed the battlefield and welcomed Palila. She knew that no one dared to get up from their prone position since it was a *kumu-kānāwai* belonging to Palila that, once prone, no one could rise again until Palila laughed. As he was a very serious young man, that didn't happen very often. Hina then undressed herself and rolled naked on the backs of the soldiers. This astonishing sight caused Palila to laugh.

Ka-lua-o-pālena and his soldiers rose and welcomed the hero who had saved them. They shouted noisily as they looked at the fallen trees, now being covered by the water from Palila's new spring, well on its way to being a lake, which is still there at Koloa.

Within ten days, a messenger came from the ruling chief of O'ahu asking Palila's help.

He had many adventures on O'ahu and Hawai'i and became the ruling chief of the Hilo district of that island. His grandmother had predicted this, and it was she who had named him Palila, after a brightly colored bird found only on the island of Hawai'i.

It was left to Lu'anu'u's son, Kūkona, to end the wars between Kona and Puna.

Kūkona

Kūkona inherited an island at war and left it united as one kingdom. From then on, the legends of the Kona kingdom were seldom told and the genealogies of the first settlers were forgotten. There were enough heroes and heroines to keep the storytellers busy with new sagas, beginning with Kūkona himself.

Kūkona's *ali'i wahine* was Lau-puapua-ma'a, and they had twin sons, Mano-ka-lani-pō and Palekaluhi.

When Kūkona became *ali'i nui* of Puna, the Kona chief was Makali'i-nui-kū-a-ka-wai-ea. He had been at the royal court of O'ahu for many years and several times had fought in battles against Kama-pua'a, who in later times became deified as a demigod who could take on many forms, especially that of a pig. Makali'i-nui-kū-a-ka-wai-ea had been the sole survivor of these battles and had been sent by Kamapua'a to the royal court with the bad news of defeat.

Eventually Makaliʻi-nui-kū-a-ka-wai-ea returned home to Waimea and organized his own forces. Makaliʻi-nui-kū-a-ka-wai-ea's army included the father and older brother of Kama-puaʻa.

Makaliʻi-nui-kū-a-ka-wai-ea went to war. The two armies met at Koloa Gap, the area between Ka-hoa-ea, the inland start of the ridge leading to Hāʻupu, and Ka-moʻo-loa, the ridge that leads to Ka-wai-kini, tallest peak on Kauaʻi. The war basically became a stalemate; neither side was stronger than the other until Limaloa and Kama-puaʻa joined the Puna army. Limaloa was a giant of a man who had become friends with Kama-puaʻa when he first came to Kauaʻi.

Kama-puaʻa dared Limaloa and Kūkona to join him in single-handed combat against any of Makaliʻi-nui-kū-a-ka-wai-ea's champions. The three advanced to the front lines and issued their challenge to take on any member of the Kona forces willing to face an individual contest.

Kahiki-ʻula, a middle-aged man, stepped forward to accept the challenge.

Kama-puaʻa said to Kūkona, "Here is your man." Kūkona, giving Kahiki-ʻula no time to prepare himself, struck Kahiki-ʻula to the ground with his war club. He was about to swing a second time to make sure the man was dead, but Kama-puaʻa stopped him. "Let me finish him off," he said. "You and Limaloa go on forward." The two warriors went in search of a new opponent. As soon as they were out of hearing, Kama-puaʻa leaned over Kahiki-ʻula. "You are almost dead," Kama-puaʻa said. "Crawl from here and return to your family in Kalalau." So Kahiki-ʻula, who was Kama-puaʻa's father, survived the battle.

Kama-puaʻa ran after his companions. They were watching a Kona warrior as he made insulting gestures and chanted a ditty concerning the lack of strength and ability of the two men in front of him. Kama-puaʻa recognized his brother, Kahiki-honua-kele. "Here is your man," Kama-puaʻa said to Limaloa who rushed upon Kahiki-honua-kele and laid him low with a blow from his war club. Limaloa was about to strike again when Kama-puaʻa stopped him. "Go on after the others," Kama-puaʻa said, "I'll finish this one off." Kahiki-honua-kele was sent back, like his father, to his home in Kalalau.

Then Kama-puaʻa came face to face with Makaliʻi-nui-kū-a-ka-wai-ea. The Kona chief did not recognize his former enemy and asked if Kama-puaʻa's name compared with his. This, of course, angered Kama-puaʻa, and he chanted a long mele listing each and every warrior he had ever defeated in battle. When he was done, Makali'i-nui-kū-a-ka-wai-ea replied:

Make.	I am defeated.
aohe wahi e ola ai,	There is no way of escape,
aohe uka,	no place in the uplands,
aohe kai,	no place in the lowlands,
aohe nae,	no place in the east,
aohe lalo,	no place underneath,
aohe opu weuweu e pee iho ai.	not even a bunch of grass for me to hide in.
ua make ia oe e Kama.	I am your captive, Kama.

The two kingdoms were merged into one with Kūkona as the *ali'i nui.* To cement the new situation, Nae-kapu-lani, the daughter of Makali'i-nui-kū-a-ka-wai-ea, was married to Kūkona's son Mano-ka-lani-pō.

Meanwhile, on the island of Hawai'i, Ka-lau-nui-o-Hua dreamed that his hand was possessed by the god Kāne-nui-akea. He had only to point his hand at an island, invade it, and the island would fall into his possession. He dreamed that he could become ruler of all the islands.

He pointed his hand at the island of Maui and defeated the Maui ruler Ka-malu-o-Hua. The Maui chief was not put to death; instead, he was appointed as governor of the island, for as governor he still commanded the loyalty of his people but took his orders from his conqueror.

Then Ka-lau-nui-o-Hua pointed to Moloka'i. Taking Ka-malu-o-Hua with him, he fought Ka-haku-o-Hua of Moloka'i, defeated him, and named him governor of the island. Taking Ka-malu-o-Hua and Ka-haku-o-Hua with him, Ka-lau-nui-o-Hua invaded O'ahu.

Hua-i-pou-leilei, ruler of O'ahu, could not defeat the forces of Hawai'i either and like the others before him found that he was a prisoner.

Ka-lau-nui-o-Hua now pointed his hand toward Kaua'i. So began the war known as Ka-welewele-iwi (*Stripping of Flesh from the Bones*).

Ka-lau-nui-o-Hua's fleet consisted of more than a thousand canoes. It seemed as though they stretched halfway across the wide channel between the two islands. When this fleet gathered off the beach of the *ahupua'a* of Māhā'ulepu, Pā'ā and Weliweli, there was no one to oppose their landing. The plains between sea and the

Hāʻupu mountain range were empty. By nightfall the entire fleet had been drawn up onto the beaches, and the army had set up camps and was resting. Ka-lau-nui-o-Hua built a house for his three prisoners and surrounded them with guards.

Kūkona had known the invasion was coming, for the guardian watchers of Hāʻupu had seen the fleet as it left Oʻahu and reported the news. These watchers were three huge stones placed along the ridges of Hāʻupu mountain, and they reported to a fourth stone located in Weliweli *ahupuaʻa*, a very sacred stone whose name is now lost.

At the news of an invasion, Kūkona first ordered every inhabitant of the land from Kīpūkai to Lāwaʻi to leave their homes, taking all the food they had with them, and move far up into the center of the island to escape the invaders. Second, he gathered all his warriors and hid them among the trees on all the ridges overlooking the seashore from Māhāʻulepu to Lāwaʻi. Third, he ordered every canoe on the island, from the large double-hulled voyaging canoes to two-man outriggers, to gather in Hanapēpē bay.

Kūkona allowed Ka-lau-nui-o-Hua to land unopposed, for he understood that if the landing was deserted, Ka-lau-nui-o-Hua would have to come looking with part of his army, leaving some to guard the canoes, thus reducing his effective fighting forces. To draw Ka-lau-nui-o-Hua far inland, Kūkona showed himself openly, standing on a nearby ridge dressed in full regalia with helmet and cape and huge royal *kāhili* (standards) towering above him. As soon as Ka-lau-nui-o-Hua headed for him, Kūkona disappeared, only to reappear on another ridge.

Ka-lau-nui-o-Hua led his troops along the lower edges of Hāʻupu range. In so doing he passed through the sacred enclosure of the guardian stone without the proper prayers and offerings. The same god that had possessed his hand, Kāne-nui-akea, was also the deity of this rock and was offended by Ka-lau-nui-o-Hua's failure. Kāne-nui-akea caused a Kauaʻi warrior, Ka-ulia, to stand up from his hiding place on the ridge and point at the invading chief. The godly power transferred to the Kauaʻi warrior.

Ka-lau-nui-o-Hua, thinking he was face to face with Kūkona, pointed back at Ka-ulia and urged his army forward, confident that he had now pointed at the Kauaʻi ruler, and the island would soon be his. It was Ka-lau-nui-o-Hua himself who was now slated for defeat.

Kūkona lured Ka-lau-nui-o-Hua farther and farther away from his canoes. Within a few hours, Ka-lau-nui-o-Hua's army was stretched out in a thin line from Māhā'ulepu to Lāwa'i. Then, at daylight on the morning after the landing, Kūkona began his attack. From the surrounding hills and ridges poured an army of ten thousand Kaua'i warriors. At the same time, speeding along the coast, came Kūkona's fleet of a thousand canoes to cut off all hope of retreat by sea.

There was time to launch some of Ka-lau-nui-o-Hua's fleet and the sea battle turned the ocean red. Standing in water to their hips, the Hawai'i forces tried to keep the Kaua'i forces from landing. Canoes were upset. Men were hauled into the Kaua'i canoes by force and killed. Enemies held onto one another and drowned together. Neither side yielded until only a handful of Hawai'i men were still alive.

Meanwhile, on land, Kūkona's troops smashed through Ka-lau-nui-o-Hua's lines and broke the opposing army into little pockets. Buffeted from front, back, and sides, the Hawai'i army broke and ran, flying in all directions. A thousand or more fought their way back to the Māhā'ulepu beach. There they climbed into any canoe they found and paddled out to sea. Some of these had too few men in them to be navigated properly and after passing through the breakers were quickly overtaken by the Kaua'i forces. Others were so heavily overloaded with men that they foundered in the surf. Not more than thirty men escaped by sea to return to Hawai'i with news of Ka-lau-nui-o-Hua's defeat.

All during this battle, Ka-lau-nui-o-Hua was conspicuous on the battlefield, but when he saw his army melting away, he realized that the battle was lost. He attempted to cut through the battlefield to make his way back to the beach. The Kaua'i chief Ka-ulia intercepted the fleeing Ka-lau-nui-o-Hua and took him prisoner.

The chiefs of Maui, Moloka'i and O'ahu were discovered. By nightfall Kūkona found himself in possession of the rulers of the four major windward islands. It was a historical moment. The five principal ruling chiefs of all the islands were gathered together in one place, four of them prisoners of the fifth. If Kūkona was ambitious enough, he could order the deaths of these chiefs and take command of their lands, thus making him the first ruler of all the islands. If he wished, he could become the ruler of a united archipelago.

Some of his chiefs urged him to do just that; others warned him of the dangers involved. While he made up his mind what to do,

Kūkona made a tour of Kauaʻi to show his guests all the beauties for which the island was, and is, famous.

When they arrived at Hale-manu in the mountains, it was raining. Kūkona decided to take a nap. He rolled himself in his tapa blankets and closed his eyes. Soon his steady breathing announced to the four captives that he had fallen asleep. The four chiefs began to talk quietly among themselves, grumbling and finding fault with Kūkona and the fate that had made them all his prisoners.

Ka-lau-nui-o-Hua suggested that this was a perfect opportunity to kill Kūkona and escape back to their islands. Hua-i-pou-leilei of Oʻahu and Ka-haku-o-Hua of Molokaʻi agreed. Ka-malu-o-Hua of Maui rejected their plan. Kūkona had been kind to them, he said, and could easily have put them to death at the time of their capture. Instead, they had been treated well and now only were waiting for ransom to be raised on their home islands before they would be freed.

Just then Kūkona sat up and stretched. "I have had an interesting dream," he said. "I dreamed that all of you were muttering and plotting my death, but Ka-malu-o-Hua defended me. I owe my life to him."

The four chiefs, taken by surprise, told him his dream was true. Then they waited for Kūkona's order to put them to death, a fate they had earned.

Kūkona, however, had no dream of being supreme ruler of all the islands. He thought only of the peace of Kauaʻi. Therefore, Kūkona said, "Because Ka-malu-o-Hua saved my life, I will free him and the other former prisoners. Ka-lau-nui-o-Hua must remain a prisoner until such time as he is ransomed. You three will return to your homes, taking your canoes with you. Your lands shall be your own to live in as before. In return, you four must swear never to invade this island again, never in your lifetime or in the lives of any of your descendants."

The four captive chiefs agreed. Kūkona ordered a *heiau* built on the brow of the long ridge that divides Alakaʻi swamp from the valleys of Nāpali. Here in this *heiau*, which they named Ka-unu-o-Hua (*Altar of the Hua*), they made their promise. This peace was called Ka-lai-loa-ia-Kamaluohua (*The Long Peace of Kamaluohua*), and it lasted more than five hundred years.

4

WĀ MAIKAʻI
Good Times

Once kauaʻi was united as one kingdom and was free from any threat of invasion from its windward neighbors, attention was focused on the development of a solid political system based on land divisions. The paramount chief ruled the entire island, owned all the land, and had the power of life and death over the people, *aliʻi* (chiefs) and *makaʻāinana* (commoners) alike. To help him govern, the *aliʻi nui* chose a *kālaimoku* (prime minister; literally: manage island) to advise him on all practical political and civil matters.

The royal establishment was kept at Wailua, although there was also a permanent home at Waimea. Chiefs and chiefesses of high rank who possibly might attract enough discontents to pose a threat were better kept at court where they could be watched while being made to feel an integral part of the kingdom. Young *aliʻi* and *makaʻāinana* men were kept as a standing army, vigorously trained in all the martial arts. To keep interest lively, these athletes displayed their skills and bravery in frequent pageants and tournaments where betting took on a punitive aspect. Genealogists, historians, storytellers, and hula troops kept the royal court entertained. A horde of commoners kept daily life operating smoothly.

Kauaʻi was divided into six *moku* (districts), which were governed by an *aliʻi ʻai moku* (chief who leads the land), each carefully chosen for his loyalty and close relationship to the ruling chief. The largest district was Kona, the former kingdom centered at Waimea, followed in size by Puna. Koʻolau, the land between the Makaleha mountains and the sea that faced the northeast trade winds, contained the least amount of water but had a teeming reef along its shores. Heleleʻa, with its spectacular mountains and waterfalls, and Nāpali of the western-facing valleys surrounded by two-thousand-foot cliffs and the open ocean, are the most spectacular. The island of Niʻihau was populated from Kauaʻi during years of sufficient rainfall and abandoned when drought beset it.

The *aliʻi ʻai moku* was responsible for the well-being of his district and for passing on to the *aliʻi nui* the prescribed amount of food, from taro to pigs, from bananas to fish. He also sent food and such manufactured necessities of life that the people in his district produced.

In addition, each of these districts was further divided into smaller pie-shaped land units called *ahupuaʻa*, reaching from a point in the mountains, down two ridges surrounding and containing a constantly flowing stream, and reaching out into the deep-sea fishing grounds offshore. The district chief appointed a *konohiki* (chief) to be in charge of each *ahupuaʻa*. The families living there had access to all the resources within the *ahupuaʻa*, including *loʻi* (taro fields) and dry-land *māla* (farming fields). In return, the *ahupuaʻa* inhabitants had to work on a fixed schedule in fields set aside for the government. Once a year the commoners paid a tax in the form of pigs, dogs, vegetables, seafood, *lauhala* mats and baskets, cordage, tools, wooden calabashes, gourd containers, and, above all, feathers from the colorful forest birds, which were used to make the cloaks, *lei*, and helmets used to indicate *aliʻi* status.

Since the *aliʻi nui* was considered the personal representative, as well as a direct descendant, of the gods on earth, it was natural that he owned all the land with all living things upon it, including the people who could not and did not own anything. The *aliʻi nui* had the awesome responsibility to perform the proper prayers and present the proper offerings to the gods to ensure the well-being of all. He was supported by his *kahuna nui* (head priest), who advised him on all religious matters. Any *aliʻi nui* who neglected his duties could and sometimes was deposed by his people and either killed or sent into permanent exile.

The genealogy of Kaua'i *ali'i* was considered the most ancient and impeccable in all the Hawaiian islands. *Ali'i* from other islands were eager to introduce the Kaua'i bloodline into their own. Kaua'i chiefs toured the Windward islands, eager for new sights and to observe the constant battles that were taking place. Kaua'i remained at peace but certain of its warriors earned heroic reputations for their deeds on other islands.

Another charm of traveling for Kaua'i chiefs was the attention paid to them by the chiefesses of other courts. A chiefess would live with a Kaua'i chief for a time, bear one or more children, then send the chief on his way, leaving his bloodline and genealogy to mingle with those of her own family on Maui and Hawai'i. Marriage to the O'ahu families was commonplace for Kaua'i's chiefesses.

It was this peaceful kingdom that Mano-ka-lani-pō inherited and helped to create. He ruled over the Golden Age of Kaua'i history.

Mano-ka-lani-pō

The long years of destruction of people, resources, and land were over. Under Mano-ka-lani-pō, more and more land was opened for agriculture, and the population flourished. Warriors became more athletes than soldiers. So peaceful was this Golden Age that Paleka-luhi, twin brother of Mano-ka-lani-pō, died in bed of old age. Such a passing was, after so many years of war, something to be noted.

O ka hiolani kana o Palekaluhi,	His is the gentle sleep of Palekaluhi,
O ka pilipilikana lua i o Mano la,	The beloved companion of Mano,
O ke koko a kewe hookahi ana	Conceived and born in one womb
Hookahi ka aa kewe o na 'lii.	One was the afterbirth of the chiefs.

The beauty of his wife, Nae-kapu-lani, was compared to the *uhi-uhi* tree that bears numerous dark red flowers on a widespread canopy. The heartwood of *uhiuhi* is almost black while the sapwood is straw colored, a particularly beautiful combination. Unlike most trees, the *uhiuhi* wood is so dense it sinks in water. Its wood was used for *pou* (house posts), a farmer's *'ō'ō* (digging tool), women's *i'e kuku* (tapa beaters), a warrior's *ihe* (spear), and *kāma'a loa* (sled runners). It was no small compliment to Nae-kapu-lani to compare her to an *uhiuhi* tree.

56

This couple had three children: Kau-maka-a-Mano, Nā-puʻu-a-Mano, and Ka-haʻi-a-Mano, all sons. Mano-ka-lani-pō also had another wife, Pūlana-ʻieʻie, but the genealogies do not say whether they had children.

So prosperous was Mano-ka-lani-pō's reign that his people pointed with pride to his scaly skin, red eyes and generally decrepit physical condition. These were due to heavy drinking of ʻawa, a narcotic. Only high chiefs could command such a supply of ʻawa as to become addicted and debilitated. Such a physical state, however, was a source of pride to his people.

Many centuries later, Captain George Vancouver, the Englishman who followed in Captain James Cook's footsteps, described a chief who was a heavy user of ʻawa: "His limbs, no longer able to support his aged and venerable person, seemed not only deserted by their former muscular strength but their substance was also entirely wasted away and the skin, now inclosing the bones only, hung loose and unattached from the joints, whilst a dry white scruff or rather scales, overspread the whole surface of his body from head to foot, tended greatly to increase the miserable and deplorable appearance of his condition."

During Mano-ka-lani-pō's time, the Mū-ʻai-maiʻa people, still living on the edges of the Alakaʻi swamp at the top of Wainiha valley, lost their kahuna nui. He had not trained anyone to replace him, and the Mū were afraid that the gods had abandoned them. They sent their kilokilo (reader of omens in the clouds of Ke-ao-melemele) to find a kahuna nui for them. This the kilokilo promised to do—either that or to find the way home to Kāne-huna-moku.

The kilokilo arrived at the heiau of Hānai-maʻa in Hāʻena, the heiau where three gods of Kahiki had landed back in the days of Laʻa-mai-Kahiki. These were Nā-maka-o-ke-ahi (Eyes of Fire), Hānai-maʻa (Habitually Fed) and Kaunu (Desire). While he was here, the local fishermen asked him to become their kilo iʻa (a man who observes fish movements from a high place and directs fishermen to the schools he observes). Interested in ocean fishing, which was new to him, the Mū kilokilo agreed, forgetting his errand.

Then Ka-ʻauʻau, the kahuna of Mano-ka-lani-pō, arrived at Hānai-maʻa. He reminded the kilokilo that he was neglecting his duty to his people and invited him to visit the court at Wailua. Mano-ka-lani-pō was pleased, thinking that he was going to add an experienced *kilo i'a* to his staff. Ka-'au'au, however, told him that the *kilo-kilo* must be sent on his way, but only after the *kilokilo* had trained someone in his knowledge, which he did.

The *kilokilo* tried to persuade Mano-ka-lani-pō and Ka-'au'au to build a *heiau* on the high peak of Pueo, but because they were still in the process of building a *heiau* they did not wish to take on another project. Realizing that he was of no further use, the Mū *kilokilo* continued his journey.

After several adventures, the *kilokilo* saw his homeland Kāne-huna-moku offshore of Miloli'i valley and managed to persuade the ruler to allow the Mū to return home. The *kilokilo* led his people to the beach at Maniniholo at Hā'ena. The island of Kāne-huna-moku came into sight, and the Mū-'ai-mai'a left Kaua'i as the Menehune had done before them.

Also during Mano-ka-lani-pō's reign, three future goddesses—all sisters—enjoyed the hospitality of Kaua'i. They came in huge voyaging canoes, possibly from their homeland in Samoa, each accompanied by a bevy of female attendants. They arrived from the west and said they had visited Nihoa and Nekkar islands as well as Ni'ihau. Their visit to Kaua'i was short, yet their adventures caught the attention of the bards. There were no longer battles with heroic warriors doing great deeds. These flaming-haired women fired the imagination and the genius of *nā haku mele* (poets) who created a magnificent saga unique to these islands.

Kapō-'ula-kina'u was the first to arrive. In time she became the goddess of hula and of poisons and black sorcery. She was also a goddess to those who were adept at healing mental diseases, since it was Kapō-'ula-kina'u who first brought the knowledge that a psychic disorder was curable.

Kapō-'ula-kina'u promised that she would find husbands for all the young women who were with her while on the island. As soon as she landed at Mānā on the southwest coast, she learned that the *konohiki* chief who greeted her was unattached. He was a handsome man, as large and strong as a giant, and she thought him a fitting mate for her companion Moe-ha'una. His name was Limaloa. He had fought beside Kamapua'a and Kūkona in the recent war that united the island as one kingdom. That evening Kapō-'ula-kina'u joined Moe-ha'una and Limaloa together.

Kapō-'ula-kina'u continued to Kōloa where she saw a woman

being savagely beaten by her husband. Kapō-ʻula-kinaʻu transformed the woman into a large dog, which turned on the man and tore out his throat. Then Kapō-ʻula-kinaʻu changed the dog back to a woman but, to save her life from her frightened neighbors, possessed her. The woman was able to tell her neighbors secret things and to make predictions. Believing her possessed by the gods, which she was, the neighbors accepted her back in their midst.

When she reached Wailua, Kapō-ʻula-kinaʻu saw a group of eight men surfboarding, a sport she enjoyed. Another young chief offered her his board and complimented her and her young women on their beauty. Kapō-ʻula-kinaʻu hardly listened, intent as she was on the eight young men she thought would be suitable mates for her companions. Kapō-ʻula-kinaʻu challenged all eight to take a young woman on their boards with them, but they refused. Kapō-ʻula-kinaʻu then challenged them to race with her, and after she had beaten them twice, the third time she called up a rogue wave and buried them in its billows, turning them to rock.

Back on shore, the first young chief invited Kapō-ʻula-kinaʻu and her entourage to his parents' home for a feast and to spend the night. After the feast, Kapō-ʻula-kinaʻu announced that she had no gift suitable as a thank-you for the hospitality except for one of her young women. She had noticed that the young chief and one of her maidens had been eyeing each other all evening. Kapō-ʻula-kinaʻu joined them together.

The young woman was Kapō-inu-kai and the young chief was Kau-maka-a-Mano, son of Mano-ka-lani-pō.

The next two future goddesses came together, Pele and Hiʻiaka-i-ka-poli-o-Pele. Pele became the fiery goddess of the Kīlauea volcano while her sister (whose name is always shortened to Hiʻiaka, even though she had at least eight sisters whose full names also began with Hiʻiaka) became a goddess of the hula.

Pele, too, landed first at Mānā. Pele was seeking a new home and safety from her older sister Nā-maka-o-ka-haʻi. As Pele toured the island she met the pig-warrior Kama-puaʻa. The two traded insults and Kama-puaʻa attempted to rape Pele but she was saved by her sister Kapo-ʻula-kinaʻu.

Kapo-ʻula-kinaʻu went on to Hanalei where she found husbands for all the rest of her women. Then she left Kauaʻi in search of a husband for herself.

Pele went on to Kēʻē at Hāʻena where she met Limaloa's brother

Lohi'au and fell in love. She dug a cave at Hā'ena to make a home for them but water filled it. She left Kaua'i, promising Lohi'au she would return for him as soon as possible. Eventually, after several battles with Nā-maka-o-ka-ha'i, she settled at the volcano Kīlauea on Hawai'i island. Then Pele sent her young sister Hi'iaka-i-ka-poli-o-Pele to fetch Lohi'au to her.

Meanwhile, when Pele did not return, Lohi'au hung himself in despair. His body was placed in a cave above Kē'ē beach and was guarded by two mo'o (lizard) sisters, Kilioe and Aka. When Hi'iaka-i-ka-poli-o-Pele and her companion Wahine-'ōma'o arrived, the two mo'o refused to let them into the cave. Hi'iaka-i-ka-poli-o-Pele turned them to stone and, with herbs and prayers, restored Lohi'au to life.

Hi'iaka sailed to Hawai'i with Lohi'au. When they arrived at Kīlauea, Hi'iaka found that Pele had broken all the promises she had made to safeguard Hi'iaka's forests and friends. She turned to Lohi'au, whom she had learned to love on their journey, and for the first time embraced him. This enraged Pele, and she covered Lohi'au with lava, killing him a second time.

Hi'iaka, having as fiery a temper as her sister, began to dig a tunnel from the sea to the fire pit at Kīlauea, but she was persuaded by her brothers to spare Pele. Hi'iaka-i-ka-poli-o-Pele told them she would never again see Pele and returned to Kaua'i where she had first met Lohi'au.

Pele's brothers, feeling Pele had been in the wrong, restored Lohi'au to life and brought him to Kaua'i. There he and Hi'iaka were reunited and spent the rest of their lives at Hā'ena.

Their story has become the most widely known of all Hawaiian legends. Pele became the goddess of volcanoes. Hi'iaka-i-ka-poli-o-Pele's hālau hula at Kē'ē still remains a magnet for all dancers.

When Mano-ka-lani-pō died, as peacefully as his twin Paleka-luhi, the new, enlarged, prosperous, and peaceful kingdom passed on to his oldest son, Kau-maka-a-Mano.

Kau-maka-a-Mano

Kau-maka-a-Mano was a hunter of the great man-eating niuhi (sharks) that swam in the rough waters off the Nāpali cliffs. It was a very dangerous sport and took great cunning, skill, and strength. Sharks provided the ideal skin for the coverings of drums, teeth for lining the edge of war clubs, and eyes for sacrifices.

Kau-maka-a-Mano, as *aliʻi nui*, was at the center of all important religious ceremonies held to ensure the well-being of his people. In certain of these ceremonies, the eating of an eye was a significant ritual. It was, for instance, a common sacrifice to Ka-hō-āliʻi, the god who owned the two axes that the priests used to cut the *ʻōhiʻa* trees used in the building of a *luakini heiau* in which human sacrifice took place.

The *kumukānāwai* of Ka-hō-āliʻi was Puʻukoāmaka-iʻa *(Hard Eyeball of a Fish)*, a reference to the human eyeball which the god preferred as an offering. From time to time, a chief might become possessed by Ka-hō-āliʻi and invoke this *kānāwai* at a time when all the lesser chiefs had gathered for a ceremony. Once the law was invoked, everyone had to look steadily at the possessed chief, no blinking, no looking away, until such time as one of these spectators had been chosen. Then this unfortunate chief had his eyes gouged out and placed in a cup of *ʻawa* and swallowed by the god-possessed chief.

Once Kau-maka-a-Mano and his friend Kaʻu-weke were fishing on the rocks of the western side of Wainiha bay. Usually both *weke* (goatfish) and big-eyed *akule* (scad) were abundant and easy to catch at this place. On this particular day the chiefs were not catching anything. Then the reason for the scarcity of fish swam into the bay, an old, huge man-eating shark that had only one eye. The other eye socket was covered with thick scar tissue.

The single eye of a half-blind shark would make a magnificent and symbolic sacrifice. With no further thought, Kau-maka-a-Mano grasped his dagger and jumped into the water to fight the shark.

Taking advantage of the shark's blind side, Kau-maka-a-Mano, who was very strong, succeeded in killing the monster. Soon after, the *weke* returned to the bay, and Kaʻu-weke caught many. That evening, Kaʻu-weke feasted on his favorite fish while Kau-maka-a-Mano ate the shark's eye.

Naturally such an event permitted more than one interpretation and so, it was related, the grandmother of the famous brothers, the *kia manu* (birdcatchers) Waʻawaʻa-iki-naʻau-ao and Waʻawaʻa-iki-naʻau-pō, expressed one morning her desire for a supper of *weke*, and so the brothers went fishing. As he was very lazy, Waʻawaʻa-iki-naʻau-ao said to his younger brother, "All the fish we catch that have two eyes are yours. You must clean and cook them all. Any fish with one eye belong to me, and I will clean and cook those."

Waʻawaʻa-iki-naʻau-pō nodded happily for he was always glad to be told clearly what he must do. As they fished, Waʻawaʻa-iki-naʻau-pō happily watched the pile of *weke* grow larger and larger.

He was equally happy when he saw a great white shark with only one eye enter the bay and swallow his hook and the fish dangling from it. Waʻawaʻa-iki-naʻau-pō handed his fishing pole to his brother. "Here is your fish with one eye," he said to the surprised Waʻawaʻa-iki-naʻau-ao, who grasped the pole as the shark swam out to sea. Waʻawaʻa-iki-naʻau-ao, too surprised to let go, was pulled off the rocks and towed out to sea so far it took the rest of the day for him to regain the shore.

That night, he refused to join Waʻawaʻa-iki-naʻao-pō and his grandmother as they feasted on *weke* and told and retold the day's delightful adventure.

Shark-hunting Kau-maka-a-Mano had two brothers, Nā-puʻu-a-Mano and Ka-haʻi-a-Mano, but nothing is known of them. Equally unknown is the effect of his *kumukānāwai* Ka-ʻai-kana-nuʻu, although its name suggests something to do with the food increase of the newly developed agricultural lands.

His *aliʻi wahine* was Kapō-inu-kai who had come to Kauaʻi in a voyaging canoe from the west with Kapō-ʻula-kinaʻu. Kau-maka-a-Mano and Kapō-inu-kai had only one child, Ka-haku-a-Kāne.

Ka-haku-a-Kāne

Ka-haku-a-Kāne possibly was named after one of the four sons of Kumuhonua, the oldest brother of Moʻikeha, the voyager from Raʻiā-tea, but there is no indication why this name was chosen from a parallel genealogy, which has now been lost. His *kumukānāwai* was named Malo-kea (*White Loincloth*). These hints raise questions that no longer can be answered.

Ka-haku-a-Kāne, like so many of his ancestors, made a grand tour of the windward islands. He was, or would be, *aliʻi nui* of Kauaʻi and had an impeccable genealogy. When he reached Maui, Kapō-nae-nae, sister of the ruler, the first Kahekili, married him. They had two children, Ka-hekili-a-Kāne and Kū-o-nā-mau-a-ino. When Ka-hekili-a-Kāne's granddaughter married Lono-a-Piʻi, the *aliʻi nui* of Maui at that time, Maui chiefs were able to connect themselves to the ancient Kauaʻi line leading backwards to Laʻa-mai-Kahiki.

When Ka-haku-a-Kāne left Maui and returned to Kauaʻi, he married Mano-kai-koʻo, like himself a grandchild of Mano-ka-lani-pō. They had a son, Kū-walu-paukū-moku.

Kū-walu-paukū-moku

His name indicates that the genealogy of the Kona kingdom had not been lost before this time. He was named after an ancestor, the son of Kū-walu-kini-akua, the first known settler of Kauaʻi. This Kūwalu genealogy had been joined to that of Laʻa-mai-Kahiki when Kū-walu-paukū-moku's great-grandfather Mano-ka-lani-pō married Nae-kapu-lani, daughter of Makaliʻi-nui-kū-a-ka-wai-ea, last ruling chief of Kona.

Kū-walu-paukū-moku was a good, wise, and liberal ruler. His *kumukānāwai* was named Pīkele-ʻula (*Small Red Quantities*), but, as usual, what the law was and the punishment it carried have been lost.

Kū-walu-paukū-moku married Hame-a-Wahaʻula, a chiefess whose genealogy has been lost. From her name, certain connotations may be made. Wahaʻula was the first *heiau* built by the Samoan priest Pāʻao after he made his first landfall in the district of Puna on Hawaiʻi island. He had left his homeland when his brother accused Pāʻao's son of eating food that had been set aside for the ruling chief. To prove his son's innocence, Pāʻao killed his son, cut open his stomach, and proved that he had not eaten the food in question. Since his son could not be brought to life again, Pāʻao left his homeland and brought his god Wahaʻula to Hawaiʻi.

Wahaʻula was so sacred it had its own *kānāwai*, the *kapu ʻenaʻena* (tabu burning with red-hot rage). If smoke from any fire lit within the temple walls fell upon anyone outside the walls, be it commoner or chief, death was the immediate penalty. There is a legend of a young chief making his first tour of Hawaiʻi. As he walked past Wahaʻula, smoke blew on him. He was immediately killed, sacrificed on the altar, and, after a time, his bones thrown into the refuse pit. His spirit called to his father to come and give his bones a proper burial. The father, with the help of his son's spirit, entered the *heiau* precincts unseen, took up his son's bones, and disposed of them where no one could use them for evil purposes.

Within Wahaʻula's enclosure was a sacred grove of trees said to contain one or more specimens of every tree growing on all the Hawaiian islands. One of these trees was a *hame*, a medium-size tree with grapelike clusters of sour but edible fruit used to dye tapa; its hard wood was used for anvils for beating *olonā* fiber.

If Hame-a-Waha'ula was a descendant of the Pā'ao line of priests, she would have passed on to her children a strong *mana*, for the line of Pā'ao was ancient and awe-inspiring.

Ka-haku-maka-paweo

There are no legends concerning the quiet and peaceful rule of Ka-haku-maka-paweo. Even his *kumukānāwai* Kahu-alamea (*Precious Guardian*) indicates the calmness of his reign.

His wife was Ka-haku-a-kukua-'ena, of whom nothing is known, although the name indicates they must have been closely related.

They had three sons: Kaile-lalāhai, 'A'a-nui-kani-a-weke, and Ka-lani-kukuma. Nothing is known of the two older brothers except their names.

He maka ia no Ka-haku-maka-paweo,	A child of Ka-haku-maka-paweo,
He maka kapu ia no Ka-lani-kukuma,	Sacred child of Ka-lani-kukuma,
Ka kaikua'ana o Kaile-lalāhai,	Older brother of Kaile-lalāhai,
O Aa-nui-kani-a-weke no Kona, no Koolau,	(Also) Aanui-kani-aweke of Kona and Koolau,
Akolu lakou a Ka-haku-maka-paweo i hanau.	Three of them were born of Ka-haku-maka-paweo.

Ka-lani-kukuma

During the time of Ka-lani-kukuma, two Kaua'i heroes, Pāka'a and Pikoi-a-'Alalā lived, and their adventures became popular tales of the storytellers.

When Keawe-nui-a-'Umi, son of Umi-a-Liloa of Hawai'i, was born he was placed in the care of Kū-a-Nu'uanu who was entrusted as the *kahu* (guardian) to raise and educate the royal youngster. Kū-a-Nu'uanu was particularly skilled in athletic sports and games and was an expert surfrider. He also became the close advisor of his chief, and was referred to as *'iwi kua mo'o* (backbone of the chief).

After many years, Kū-a-Nu'uanu toured all the islands, leaving his charge behind. Kū-a-Nu'uanu eventually came to Kapa'a where he met Laʻa-maomao, a descendent of the navigator of the same name who had helped Moʻikeha, the traveler from Raʻiātea, win his wife many years before. Laʻa-maomao had inherited the calabash of winds as well as the name of her ancestor. Kū-a-Nuʻuanu and Laʻa-maomao settled down on a bluff overlooking the sea between Kapaʻa and Keʻālia.

After six months, word came from Hawaiʻi that Keawe-nui-a-ʻUmi wanted Kū-a-Nuʻuanu to return and take up his duties once again. Before he left Kapaʻa, Kū-a-Nuʻuanu gave his pregnant wife a white *malo* and a cape woven of *kalukalu*, a grass that grew only at Kapaʻa. If their child-to-be was a boy, she was to give him these items when he was old enough to seek out his father. When Kū-a-Nuʻuanu saw these tokens, he would recognize his son.

After Kū-a-Nuʻuanu left, Laʻa-maomao and her brother Maʻilou, a birdcatcher, raised her son. He was named Pākaʻa, as his father had requested, for the name recalled Keawe-nui-a-ʻUmi's scaly and cracked skin caused by drinking *ʻawa*. Because he had no father, Pākaʻa was teased and shunned. Indeed the three of them, mother, uncle, child, often went hungry because no one would help them.

As a youth Pākaʻa desired more than anything to eat his fill of flying fish *(mālolo)*. He carefully watched the eight-man fishing canoes as they threaded their way along the narrow channel that zigzagged across the reef. As he watched day after day, he planned a scheme to trick those fishermen of their load of *mālolo*.

He knew these fishermen were compulsive gamblers. He would challenge them to a race, eight against one, odds no gambler could resist. His *waʻa koʻo kahi* (small one-man canoe) was lighter than the *waʻa koʻo ʻewalu* (eight-man canoe) and could skim over the reef, ignoring the channel. Yet that was not enough. He needed more speed. One day he watched his mother trying to drape a sheet of tapa over a drying rack in the stiff trade wind. The wind, he realized, worked as well for a canoe with a small sail as it did for the giant traveling canoes. He created a sail in the shape of a crab's claw, small enough so that it could be handled by one man.

When he had practiced with his new sail, Pākaʻa paddled out to the deep-sea fishing ground. When he saw one canoe so filled with *mālolo* that it was low in the water, Pākaʻa challenged the crew to a race to shore. The fishermen laughed and refused. He was one, they pointed out, and they were eight, and besides he had nothing with which to bet. When Pāka'a bet his life on the outcome of the race, the fishermen agreed. His life against their load of fish.

The eight fishermen began paddling for shore while Pāka'a took his time putting up his mast and sail. Then he quickly outsailed his opponents, landed first on the beach, and won his bet and a feast of *mālolo*.

After he had grown up, Pāka'a asked his mother who his father was and where he could be found. La'a-maomao told him of Kū-a-Nu'uanu and how he was guardian and backbone of a ruling chief. Pāka'a knew he would seek out his father, but first he needed to educate himself in the ways of ruling chiefs.

So when Ka-lani-kukuma announced he was going on a trip around the island, Pāka'a decided to attach himself to the entourage to learn what the duties of the *'iwi kua mo'o* were in regards to the care and feeding of a ruling chief. Pāka'a made himself useful and learned all he could, even though he often went hungry because no one paid any attention to him.

When Ka-lani-kukuma decided to make a grand tour of all the islands, Pāka'a once again attached himself to the group. When they reached Waipi'o on Hawai'i, Ka-lani-kukuma met with Keawe-nui-a-'Umi. Pāka'a learned that Kū-a-Nu'uanu was also there, always with his chief within sacred grounds. Pāka'a put on his white *malo* and *kalukalu* cloak, ran past the guards and threw himself onto the lap of Kū-a-Nu'uanu, who immediately recognized his son. Kū-a-Nu'uanu began to train Pāka'a as *'iwi kua mo'o* of Keawe-nui-a-'Umi.

When Kū-a-Nu'uanu died, Pāka'a took his place as the favorite friend of Keawe-nui-a-'Umi. He was given large tracts of land and became the principal navigator of Keawe-nui-a-'Umi's canoe. Two men who were also excellent navigators, Ho'okele-i-Hilo and Ho'o-kele-i-Puna, became jealous and hatched a plot to discredit Pāka'a. One by one they reported little slanders and boasted of their own skills. Eventually Keawe-nui-a-'Umi favored these two, began to take away Pāka'a's land, and installed the two schemers as his principal navigators.

Pāka'a gathered a few of his chief's articles of clothing and, taking the calabash of winds, sailed away. He came to the south coast of Moloka'i and made his home there at Kau-manamana. He married Hikauhi, daughter of Ho'olehua and his wife, 'Īloli. Hikauhi died giving birth to a son, Kū-a-Pākaʻa. As his son grew, Pākaʻa taught him everything he knew and trained him to help restore Pākaʻa to favor and to obtain the death of his enemies.

When Keawe-nui-a-ʻUmi finally realized that his new favorites were not giving him the service Pākaʻa had, he decided to find his former steward. He ordered a fleet of canoes gathered and had a special double-hulled canoe built for himself. His canoe makers went into the forests, but each time they started to cut down a tree, two birds would fly in and peck at the trunk, indicating the wood was rotten and unfit for a canoe. This happened every time a seemingly acceptable tree was found. Eventually the priests announced these were supernatural birds who had the power to rot any tree they chose. Keawe-nui-a-ʻUmi sent out word that anyone who could kill these birds would be given one of his daughters as a wife. This attracted the famed archer of Oʻahu, Maʻilele, as well as the obscure Pikoi-a-ʻAlalā of Kauaʻi.

Pikoi-a-ʻAlalā had been born and raised on the plains of Kapaʻa. His great companion was Puapua-lenalena, an unusual dog with a fluffy tail, with one blue and one green eye. The dog had floated ashore in a canoe with a man who could not speak the local language. The boy and dog roamed the plains seeking out rats until such time as Pikoi-a-ʻAlalā became so proficient, it was claimed he could shoot a rat through its whiskers.

On the eagerly anticipated day, Maʻilele missed the supernatural birds but Pikoi-a-ʻAlalā shot them both through the neck with the same arrow. The canoe building continued without further incident.

When his new canoe had been properly outfitted, Keawe-nui-a-ʻUmi set sail. As he neared Molokaʻi, he came across an old man and his young son out fishing. These were Pākaʻa and his son Kū-a-Pākaʻa, but Keawe-nui-a-ʻUmi did not recognize them.

The boy told Keawe-nui-a-ʻUmi that if he continued on his journey, his fleet of canoes would be destroyed in a storm. It was a clear day with the sun sparkling on the waves, and the chief's navigators, Hoʻokele-i-Hilo and Hoʻokele-i-Puna, said there was no danger of a storm.

As soon as the fleet had entered the Oʻahu channel, Kū-a-Pākaʻa opened Laʻa-maomao's calabash and called up many winds from all the islands. He created a huge tempest, and the fleet was heavily damaged and came limping back to Molokaʻi. Accepting the hospitality of the man and boy, whom he still failed to recognize, Keawe-nui-a-'Umi put together a new fleet and continued his search for Pāka'a.

Kū-a-Pāka'a went with him. Off the coast of Kaua'i, he opened his wind calabash once again to create a terrible storm, in the course of which the two evil navigators lost their lives. Then Kū-a-Pāka'a revealed who he was and brought Keawe-nui-a-'Umi safely back to Moloka'i, where Keawe-nui-a-'Umi warmly greeted his former friend and invited him to return to Hawai'i and resume his former position. Pāka'a refused to leave Moloka'i, saying he was now too old, and instead his son, Kū-a-Pāka'a, became the 'iwi kua mo'o, the backbone of Keawe-nui-a-'Umi.

The wife of Ka-lani-kukuma was Kapō-lei-a-kuila, a direct descendant of Haulani-nui-ai-ākea, the oldest son of the seafaring Mo'i-keha. This union of the two lines after ten generations increased the mana and aristocratic rank of their two sons, Ka-haku-maka-lina and 'Ili-hiwa-lani.

Ka-haku-maka-lina became the ali'i nui after his father, but within a few generations, the ali'i of Kaua'i successfully searched for a ruler among the descendants of 'Ili-hiwa-lani.

Ka-haku-maka-lina

Unknown and unannounced to the latest Kaua'i ali'i nui, Ka-haku-maka-lina, a well-known chief of Hawai'i island, Lono-i-ka-maka-hiki, arrived on Kaua'i. He had just defeated Kama-lālā-walu of Maui in a war that ended with great destruction of the Maui forces, and Lono-i-ka-makahiki felt that they were no longer a problem. Leaving his lands in the care of his wife, he went off to Kaua'i to see the famous trunkless koa tree of Ka-hiki-kolo, a tree from which earlier warriors had fashioned war clubs.

Lono-i-ka-makahiki landed at Waimea and with his retinue in tow started out for Ka-hiki-kolo. The way was long, and the rough path constantly forded rushing streams bounding down steep walled canyons. Worse still, Lono-i-ka-makahiki did not have a guide nor had he made provisions for food and shelter. The retinue began to slip away and turn back to Waimea. Soon Lono-i-ka-makahiki found only one man was following him, a stranger to him. He was a Kaua'i man, Ka-pa'ihi-a-hilina.

Lono-i-ka-makahiki continued on his way, although he did not know where Ka-hiki-kolo was. He just blundered on with a respectful Ka-pa'ihi-a-hilina behind him. The Kaua'i chief was careful never to step on Lono-i-ka-makahiki's shadow as that would be extremely disrespectful. He observed all the protocol and deference due a high chief. For the first few nights, Ka-paʻihi-a-hilina fed Lono-i-ka-makahiki from a calabash of *poi* with some *ʻoʻopu* fish he had thought to bring along. After a few days of this treatment, Lono-i-ka-makahiki released all *kapu* and took Ka-paʻihi-a-hilina as a full and equal companion.

They wandered and the food ran out. Ka-paʻihi-a-hilina fixed a meal of ripe pandanus fruit, a food for the time of famine, but it filled their stomachs. They climbed into the mountains and their *malo* disintegrated in the rain. Ka-paʻihi-a-hilina braided soft ferns into garments for them to wear. He also wove coats of *ti* leaves to keep them from the cold and the rain.

Eventually Lono-i-ka-makahiki saw the trunkless *koa* tree and crossed Haleleʻa district from east to west. He and his companion climbed Mauna-hina ridge out of Wainiha valley and crossed the great and dangerous Alakaʻi swamp to return to Waimea. Here Lono-i-ka-makahiki found his retinue, climbed aboard his canoe and returned to Hawaiʻi, taking Ka-paʻihi-a-hilina with him. Ka-paʻihi-a-hilina became Lono-i-ka-makahiki's right-hand man to the consternation and jealousy of the Hawaiʻi chiefs. These envious men slandered Ka-paʻihi-a-hilina and whispered falsehoods in Lono-i-ka-makahiki's ears. He paid no attention until they whispered that Ka-paʻihi-a-hilina was having an affair with Lono-i-ka-makahiki's wife. Lono-i-ka-makahiki was extremely jealous and immediately believed the lies to be true.

That day, Ka-paʻihi-a-hilina returned from a fishing trip to find the entrance to the royal enclosure barred against him. Ka-paʻihi-a-hilina realized what had happened and lifted his voice in a chant to remind Lono-i-ka-makahiki of the adventures they had gone through together.

Walea kanaka i ka helea hoi mai,	The server went forth in peace, and upon returning,
He lalo ino, he laloakiaki ka ko muli nei,	He found trouble, a backbiting among inferiors,
Eia mamuli ka ukali kaeleele,	About the dark-skinned man who had followed you,
Kepai ka hookuke a.	The favorite, who is being banished.
He nani nei hele, ua hookuke oe,	It is well that I should go, for you have sent me away,

Eia la ka hewa o ka noho hale.	The owner of the house has found fault with me.
O ka noho a ku ae haalele,	Had I stayed and then gone away without cause,
Loaa la kou kina ilaila,	That would have been wrong of me,
Ko ka ohua ukali ino a.	Your companion, who followed you in stormy weather.
Aloha a haalele ia oe ke hele nei.	Farewell, I leave you and go.

Lono-i-ka-makahiki heard the chant and realized that Ka-paʻihi-a-hilina had always acted with the utmost care toward him. He ordered the gate opened, but Ka-paʻihi-a-hilina had already left. Messengers sped after him, begging him to return. Ka-paʻihi-a-hilina refused until those who had slandered him were dead. Lono-i-ka-makahiki immediately ordered their deaths, and Ka-paʻihi-a-hilina spent the rest of his life faithfully serving his chief.

The adventures of Ka-pakohana also occurred in the time of Ka-haku-maka-lina, and the hero of this story may indeed be this very chief. Ka-pakohana went to Maui to test his strength against the great strength of the Hana champion Ka-lae-hina. They were evenly matched in wrestling skills, and neither could get an advantage over the other. They seized each other in a tight grip, not daring to let go. In the struggle, Ka-pakohana maneuvered Ka-lae-hina to the edge of a cliff above the ocean. Ka-pakohana pushed them both over the edge and never let go of his opponent. Ka-lae-hina drowned while Ka-pakohana survived, since he was able to hold his breath longer than the Maui champion.

On Ka-pakohana's return to Wailua, he found that a cannibal from the valley of Hanakāpiʻai was killing new victims for his appetite. Mindful that Hawaiʻi-loa, the legendary voyager, had long ago warned against the evil of cannibalism, and that there was even a *kumukānāwai* against it named Papa-ʻenaʻena, Ka-pakohana immediately challenged the cannibal to individual combat. The Wailua chief and the cannibal were evenly matched in strength and skills. After a long battle and knowing he was tiring, Ka-pakohana offered his friendship to the cannibal who, not skilled in the ways of devious men, agreed.

That night, as the cannibal slept, Ka-pakohana ordered the sleeping house covered with fishing nets so that when the house was set on fire the cannibal could not escape. The noise of their voices and the sounds of the nets being put in place awoke the cannibal. He quietly broke open a hole in the roof and climbed out onto the ridge-pole. As soon as he understood what was happening, the cannibal climbed down with the help of a nearby *kukui* tree and killed two men. Then he and Ka-pakohana fought again for many hours, the story goes, until Ka-pakohana finally pinned the cannibal down long enough to seize his war club and bash in the cannibal's head. Ka-pakohana used the cannibal's eyes as bait for shark fishing, his long bones as hooks to hold calabashes, and the rest of his body was laid on an altar as a sacrifice to the gods.

Ka-haku-maka-lina made a grand tour of the windward islands. Everywhere he was greeted warmly. When he reached the island of Hawai'i, he was feted by 'Akahi-'ili-kapu, a daughter of 'Umi-a-Liloa. When it was time for him to return home, 'Akahi-'ili-kapu sailed to Wailua with Ka-haku-maka-lina. There she gave birth to two children, Ke-li'i-ohiohi, a son, and Koihalauwailaua, a daughter. 'Akahi-'ili-kapu returned to Hawai'i with her children, and eventually they married into the Hawai'i *ali'i* line, thus adding the Kaua'i genealogical *mana* to the descendants of 'Umi-a-Liloa.

Ka-haku-maka-lina also married Ka-haku-mai'a, a Kaua'i chiefess, whose name indicates that she too was a descendent of Ka-haku-maka-paweo. They had a son, Kama-kapu.

Kama-kapu

When Kama-kapu became *ali'i nui* of Kaua'i, the ruler of O'ahu was Kā-kuhi-hewa, who had earned a fierce reputation as a warrior, statesman, and keeper of the most glorious court in all the islands. By this time he was an old man. For his fourth wife, he chose a young Kaua'i chiefess, Ka-hā-malu-'ihi.

She had an impeccable genealogy descending, on her mother's side, from 'Ili-hiwa-lani, second son of Ka-lani-kukuma. From her father, Kawelo-'ehu, she was a direct descendant of Ahukini-a-La'a, thus giving her a double-looped genealogy, making her *mana* the strongest on Kaua'i. She owned three very powerful *kumukānāwai*.

From her grandfather Ke-'alohi-kīkaupe'a she had inherited the *kapu puhi kanaka*, the right to burn anyone to death who broke any of her *kapu* or *kānāwai*. In addition, she had the Kaihehe'e and the Lumalumai, both of which carried a dreadful punishment. The law-breaker was tied hand and foot and placed in a long fishing trap, which was then laid out on a reef at low tide. As the tide came in, the victim slowly drowned.

Ka-hā-malu-ʻihi came from the sacred sands of Waimea on the southern coast of Kauaʻi and her lands there became a *puʻuhonua* (place of refuge) for those who had broken her laws. If the law-breaker could step upon these particular sands, even the dreaded chiefess could not follow for fear of provoking the gods.

She and her brother Ke-aka-Kanaloa were two of the seven "kite flying" children of Hoʻohila, although what that meant is no longer known. Hoʻohila was the name of Ka-hā-malu-ʻihi's grandmother (wife of Ke-ʻalohi-kipaupea of Oʻahu) as well as that of a cave on the shore of Lumahaʻi *ahupuaʻa*.

Hoʻohila was a *moʻo* maiden in charge of the narrow path on the shore of Lumahaʻi *ahupuaʻa*. This path crept around the cliff that led from Waikoko *ahupuaʻa*. If Hoʻohila liked the looks of the traveler, she kept the waves low, but if she decided she did not like the traveler's appearance, she caused large waves to sweep across the path, break against the cliff, and recede, taking the path with them. When Hiʻiaka-i-ka-poli-o-Pele and her friend Wahine-ʻōmaʻo tried to pass, Hoʻohila sent the large waves. Wahine-ʻōmaʻo threw a handful of sand in Hoʻohila's eyes, the *moʻo* retired to her cave, and the waves receded. She was one of the few *moʻo* to escape being killed by Hiʻiaka-i-ka-poli-o-Pele.

Ka-hā-malu-ʻihi is frequently called Ka-lua-o-Hoʻohila in chants, which has caused confusion in certain genealogists who think Ka-hā-malu-ʻihi and Ka-lua-o-Hoʻohila are two separate women.

Genealogically this chiefess was more than a match for the elderly Kā-kuhi-hewa, who died shortly after their marriage. Then she married Kāne-kapu-a-Kā-kuhi-hewa, Kā-kuhi-hewa's son, and with him had Ka-hoʻowaha-o-ka-lani. Although she herself never ruled Kauaʻi, her influence on the history of the island is immense, for three generations later, her great-grandson Kūaliʻi became, in his turn, the *aliʻi nui* of Kauaʻi. He had inherited his claim to Kauaʻi through her and her three dreadful *kumukānāwai*.

Of Kama-kapu himself nothing is known. There are no great adventures, no notable heroes who have left their trace.

All that is known is that Kama-kapu married Pā-wahine and they had one son, Kawelo-mahamaha-iʻa.

With the birth of that son, the peaceful years were over.

5

KAUA
War

THE CENTURIES OF PREOCCUPATION WITH RANK AND MANA, THE inheritance of *kumukānāwai* that culminated in the deadly combination held by Ka-hā-malu-'ihi, which everyone, commoners and chiefs alike, had to obey, took an ominous turn. A new rank of *mana* called *ni'aupi'o* came into being with the birth of twins begotten by a brother and sister.

The ancient wisdom was that the offspring of such a union would have stronger *mana* than anyone else living and thus hold higher rank. The *ni'aupi'o* automatically carried the *kapu moe*, which meant that anyone entering that chief's presence must do so crawling on one's stomach. Any commoner must fall to his or her face whenever the chief, or any article belonging to that chief, passed by. If the *ni'aupi'o's* shadow fell on any person or any object, living or inanimate, it immediately became sacred and was destroyed. For this reason, unless elaborate ceremonies freed them from the *kapu* for a short time and specific purpose, *ni'aupi'o* only moved about at night.

The legends offer no explanation, no answer to the question: Why was the *ni'aupi'o* created at this time?

Kawelo-mahamaha-i'a

It was Kawelo-mahamaha-i'a, son of Kama-kapu and Pā-wahine, who made the fateful decision to create once again a child who bore the *ni'aupi'o* rank. Had Kawelo-mahamaha-i'a been humiliated by having to obey his cousin Ka-hā-malu-'ihi, whose *kapu* was stronger than his? Did he wish to humiliate her in turn, for she, too, would have to fall prone on the ground before a *ni'aupi'o* chief.

It was an easy thing to do. Kawelo-mahamaha-i'a and his wife Ka-pōhina-o-ka-poko had six children. Their last two were a boy, Kawelo-maka-lua, and a girl, Ka-'āwihi-a-ka-lani, both still young and still virgin. Together they could produce a child that would have the *ni'aupi'o* rank who would carry the *kapu moe*.

As soon as it was possible, the youngsters were mated. When Ka-'āwihi-o-ka-lani became pregnant, the island was searched for other women who were pregnant and might give birth at the same time. They found that the chiefess Ka-'ena-kū-o-ka-lani of Hanalei and Ka-'āwihi-o-ka-lani's older sister Malai-a-ka-lani also were pregnant. The three women were gathered at the birthstones of Holoholokū to wait. When Ka-'āwihi-o-ka-lani's birth pangs began, Kawelo-maha-maha-i'a imposed a *kapu* of deep silence over the land. The gods did not listen.

Kawelo	Kawelo
O ke 'lii nona ka hakikili	The chief whose sacred edict
Haki apana apana i Holoholoku ke kapu.	Was broken and ignored at Holoholokū.
O ke kapu mai hoana e hoomehameha,	The sacredness which should have caused silence
O ka pehea hoi o na leo kawakawa i ka po;	Was disregarded by the sound of many voices in the night;
I lani ka eloelo i ka lele mai polua;	By the sound of the gentle rain of heaven;
Io nahae nahae mai o lele;	By the rending of wet tapa in the heavy rains;
I na pu kolukolu i ke kolukolu ia iku lani.	By the loud reverberating sound of the heavens.

As Ka-'awihi-o-ka-lani began labor, her sister Malai-a-ka-lani was administered medicines to hasten the birth of her child. The birth of Ka-'ena-kū-o-ka-lani's child was held back for several hours.

As the storm raged outside the sacred enclosure of Holoholokū, Ka-'awihi-o-ka-lani gave birth. Not only were the gods roaring their approval of this *ni'aupi'o* birth, but they doubled its importance, for there was not just one *ni'aupi'o,* but two, twin boys.

The firstborn, Kawelo-pe'ekoa, was taken by the priests to be raised in seclusion as the supreme *ali'i kapu.*

The second born, Kawelo-'ai-kanaka, was raised to become ruler.

Malai-a-ka-lani that same day gave birth to her fourth child and named him Kawelo-lei-makua. Ka'ena-kū-o-ka-lani also gave birth to a boy, Ka-uahoa, but his birth had been deliberately delayed and she died in childbirth, the first sacrifice to the new *ni'aupi'o* rank.

In the legends, Kawelo-'ai-kanaka is always referred to as 'Aikanaka. His first cousin Kawelo-lei-makua is always called Kawelo.

The birth of *ni'aupi'o* twins caused an immediate problem: No one knew the rules or how to behave. To ease the twins' isolation, Kawelo and Ka-uahoa were given the rank of *wohi,* which meant they could move more or less freely in the presence of their *hoa-hānau* (birth-brothers) and be companions and playmates for the twins. Ka-uahoa, who was a large boy and in time referred to as a giant, stood always at 'Aikanaka's right hand. Kawelo-lei-makua and 'Aikanaka took an immediate and strong dislike to each other. 'Aikanaka thought of himself as a god on earth, Kawelo knew he was human and a pretty unpleasant specimen at that.

As these children grew, the island prospered under Kawelo-mahamaha-i'a. Peace continued to prevail, and he undertook to expand the land under cultivation as the population grew. Kaua'i became an island of plenty, and its hospitality was renowned throughout the archipelago.

Kawelo-mahamaha-i'a built two *heiau.* One bears his name and was constructed at the coast of Ka-malo-malo'o *ahupua'a.* The other, named 'Aikanaka, was raised nearby. Both are near the present-day town of Anahola. These *heiau* were of the *luakini* class, which meant that human sacrifices were offered there, usually of those who had broken the new *kapu.*

Remembering that the great hero Palila once killed a man after exposing a huge shark's mouth on his back, people rumored that

Kawelo-mahamaha-iʻa was such a shark-man *kupua*. His name suggested as much; Kawelo-mahamaha-iʻa can be translated as "The motion of the gills of a fish." The rumors grew.

People whispered that Kawelo-mahamaha-iʻa, as he was going to Anahola or back to Wailua, would go down to the shore, dive into the sea, and change into a large white shark. Speeding into any group of swimmers, surfers, or fishermen along his path, he ate his fill. Then the great white shark would swim up the Wailua river to the junction of the north and south forks and enter his shark's house, a large rock on the riverbed. He would then become human again and climb onto the bank to enter a large house-shaped rock on the bank. These were Nā-hale-o-Kawelo-mahamaha-iʻa (The Houses of Kawelo-mahamaha-iʻa). These rocks are still visible.

As deaths continued and sacrifices grew frequent, fear grew into anger. Finally, as he traveled back from Anahola one day, Kawelo-mahamaha-iʻa was stoned to death.

Kawelo-maka-lua

Kawelo-maka-lua, father of the *niʻaupiʻo* twins, was a thoughtful and considerate ruler in contrast to the cruelty of his father and his son. Past and future events completely overshadow his time as *aliʻi nui*, and he obviously did not live long as ruling chief.

Kawelo-ʻai-kanaka

ʻAikanaka was the *niʻaupiʻo*; his rank and power were awesome, but Kawelo was never impressed. Kawelo sought every opportunity to tease his cousin, for example, interrupting prayers by imitating a mudhen, for the cry of an *ʻalae* announced the unwillingness of the gods to listen to more of the prayer. He played practical jokes in full view of the commoners who laughed silently and took Kawelo deeply into their hearts, something ʻAikanaka never could do. Kawelo was not afraid of ʻAikanaka, but he was wary of Ka-uahoa, the other boy born that fateful night at Holoholokū. Ka-uahoa was much larger, and stronger for one thing, than Kawelo. Kawelo challenged Ka-uahoa to contest after contest, hoping one day to win against this giant playmate. He never did but he never stopped trying.

To keep him out of mischief, so they hoped, his guardians gave Kawelo a small canoe and day after day he would paddle up and down the Wailua river. Ka-uahoa was jealous and demanded that his guardians make him a canoe, too. They themselves were not happy with the rivalry between the boys and said, "It is better that you do not challenge Kawelo in this way. We will make you a kite instead." Ka-uahoa's guardians made him a kite, and while Kawelo paddled, Ka-uahoa's kite soared overhead.

Now Kawelo grew jealous and demanded that his guardians make him a kite, which they did. Kawelo joined Ka-uahoa on the banks of the Wailua river, and the two kites soared into the sky. In little jerks, Kawelo maneuvered his kite next to that of Ka-uahoa and entangled cords connecting the boys to the kites. The cords broke and the entangled kites flew off to crash on the ridge near Hā'upu mountain peak. Kawelo braced himself, for he expected Ka-uahoa to throw himself upon the transgressor in a fury. But Ka-uahoa merely walked away. In that moment Kawelo lost his fear of Ka-uahoa.

'Aikanaka never lost an opportunity to humiliate Kawelo. Kawelo was called *po'o nui, maka a'a* (big head with fiery eyes) and *moa kāne* (rooster) since he was a little fellow compared to the others. Kawelo took these names to himself. Big head with defiant eyes, he said of himself. The Rooster name he enjoyed.

He paa kaua au na aaaua a moa,	I am as skilled at war as an old tough rooster,
Ua pii kakala, akaakaa ka hulu!	Whose spurs stick out, bristling with rage!
Ke kau ana oia Moa la!	Here stands Rooster!
Mahi ia Moa!	Strong is Rooster!

Soon Kawelo had a younger brother, Ka-malama. The two were inseparable. They were raised together by their paternal grandparents who trained the youngsters in all the arts and crafts needed by the *ali'i* of those days. In every endeavor Kawelo worked hard to outdo his *hoahānau*, those three boys born the same night as he.

The spats and quarrels among the birth brothers continued throughout their childhood. The enmity exploded when the boys became young men and the time came for them to be instructed in the arts of love. It was the custom that high-ranking youngsters would be taken by an older, experienced chiefess who would teach them what they needed to know. A chiefess' name might be put forward but the choice, both of the experience and the youngster, was entirely hers. Her favors had to be won.

The chiefess Ka-aka-ukuhi-ma-lani waited for Kawelo and 'Aikanaka to woo her. Kawelo, of course, saw this as a contest, a way to get the better of 'Aikanaka once again. He, at the advice of his grandparents, tried to dazzle the chiefess with his knowledge of farming, but she didn't find that interesting and looked on 'Aikanaka more favorably. Kawelo tried to interest her in his knowledge of fishing, but that was no more successful than his reputation as a farmer. Ka-aka-ukuhi-ma-lani gave a feast, and Kawelo, no longer hopeful, went to it and danced a series of *hula*, some solemn, some comic, some erotic. He danced his way into the chiefess's heart.

'Aikanaka of course was furious. He, too, gave a feast. During the meal, three friends of 'Aikanaka picked up the huge *poi* calabash from the middle of the table and up-ended it over Kawelo's head. The audience roared with laughter and Kawelo knew the stings of deep humiliation. He made up his mind to leave Kaua'i and join his relatives on O'ahu where, he hoped, he would find more congenial living.

Kawelo and his brother Ka-malama settled on land given him at Halemanu at the foot of Ka'ala mountain. The two often crossed the pass into Wai'anae to enjoy the ocean. During these activities, two young chiefs, Ka-lau-meki of Wai-'anae and Ka-'ele-hā-o-Puna of 'Ewa, caught Kawelo's eye, and he adopted them as his sons. Kawelo also saw a champion surfer, Kāne-wahine-iki-aoha, fell in love with her, and successfully wooed her. Her father was Kalona-i-ka-hai-lā'au, an expert in the use of the various strokes of different war weapons. Under his training, Kawelo became an expert in the use of the war club and Kāne-wahine-iki-aoha became an expert in the use of the *pikoi*.

He also found a fisherman of Wai'anae, Makuakeke, and used him as a guide to find the famous fish Uhu-māka'ika'i, a huge supernatural fish, a *kupua* that had been caught once by Limaloa of the Mānā mirage. One evening after a frustrating day searching for this illusive fish, Kawelo had a vision. He saw that the peaks of Hā'upu and Ka-lani-moku were on fire and saw his parents flying like birds down the face of Hā'upu.

The following day, two men came from Kaua'i with the message that 'Aikanaka had stripped Kawelo's parents, Malai-a-ka-lani and Ma'i-huna-li'i, of everything they owned until they had been reduced to eating the lice in their hair. Their final refuge had been the *heiau* on the top of Hā'upu where 'Aikanaka laid siege to them. When the *heiau* finally surrendered, 'Aikanaka had his aunt and uncle thrown from the top of the mountain.

The two messengers were Kawelo's uncles. They came to Oʻahu, they said, to bring Kawelo back to Kauaʻi so that he could wage war on ʻAikanaka and take over the governing of the island. Kawelo accepted the challenge.

He borrowed a war canoe and twenty-four warriors from Ka-ʻihi-kapu, ruling chief of Oʻahu. Ka-ʻihi-kapu waved away payment, asking only that if Kawelo succeeded in killing ʻAikanaka and he died himself during the coming war, the rulership of the island would pass to Ka-ʻihi-kapu or to his heir. Kawelo agreed.

He and his wife, Kāne-wahine-iki-aoha, went to his father-in-law for last-minute instructions in the use of their weapons. Kalona-i-ka-hai-lāʻau refused to help and Kawelo angrily challenged his teacher to a fight. Kalona-i-ka-hai-lāʻau, who had kept back one of the war club strokes for just such an emergency, agreed. The fight, however, was quickly over. Kawelo stood over his fallen father-in-law and cried out his war chant for the first time.

Make akula oe ia Kuikaa—ia hookaa!	You have been felled by Kuikaa, the avenger!
Ka mea e wali ai ke kapukupuku.	The war club that grinds up the rock foundation.
Eia mai ka moa i hanaina la!	Here is the rooster fed in the sun!
Hookahi no peku, puko wale!	A single kick, and you are driven off!

With the twenty-four Oʻahu warriors, the twelve Ulu warriors who were part of Kawelo's entourage, his adopted sons Ka-lau-meki and Ka-ʻele-hā-o-Puna, his brother Ka-malama and his wife, Kāne-wahine-iki-aoha, accompanied by his war god, Kāne-i-ka-pua-lena, and his uncles, Kawelo set sail for Wailua. With this small group, Kawelo rode the waves onto Wailua beach, into the heart of ʻAikanaka's territory.

When he heard that his uncles had gone to Oʻahu to bring Kawelo back, ʻAikanaka retired to a *heiau* on the top of Nounou (Sleeping Giant) mountain. He gathered his fighting force around him but forgot to send a message to Ka-uahoa, the most famous of his fighters. When ʻAikanaka saw a double canoe slide onto the beach below, he sent his messenger Ka-ʻehu-iki-ʻawa-kea down to find out the purpose of the visit.

Ka-ʻehu-iki-ʻawa-kea climbed aboard, and when he found that Ka-malama was the leader of the group, he laughed.

"Where is Kawelo?" he asked.

"On O'ahu," Ka-malama lied, for Kawelo was wrapped in a tied-up *lauhala* mat. The messenger saw it, kicked it once or twice, and thought no more about it.

Ka-malama then asked that he and his crew be allowed to come ashore, wash off their salt-encrusted skins, and eat. Only then, he said, would they be ready to fight. Permission was given, for already the beach was crowded with the men belonging to two of 'Aikanaka's champions, Ka-ahu-ulu and Onioni-kaua. These champions ordered their men to carry the canoe further inland. Once the canoe had been lifted and carried across the land, Ka-malama cut the cords freeing Kawelo. Kawelo stood up with his war club Ku'i-ka'a in hand.

Nearby spectators recognized Kawelo and called out a warning but too late. With a sweep of Ku'ika'a, Kawelo mowed down the men on the left side of the canoe and with another sweep of his deadly shark-toothed weapon felled men on the right side. Some of the Wailua men were so frightened to see Kawelo that they ran away. Kawelo's warriors leapt to the sand and fought the enemy. In a few minutes, Onioni-kaua and Ka-ahu-ulu lay dead.

As soon as he saw these champions die, Ka-'ehu-iki-'awa-kea ran up Nounou, followed by Ka-malama, who tore off the messenger's *malo* and drew a scratch down his back with a dagger. The nude and terrified messenger told 'Aikanaka the bad news.

'Aikanaka sent two of his chiefs, Ka-ihu-pepe-nui-a-mouo and Muno, with their men down to the beach. Ka-'ehu-iki-'awa-kea saw these two fall in the onslaught led by Ka-malama and returned to 'Aikanaka with this fearful news. 'Aikanaka ordered another of his chiefs, Kū-ahi-lau, to take, the legend says, eight hundred men and bring Kawelo as a prisoner back to him.

Seeing this imposing group coming toward him, Kawelo set his men into three divisions. Ka-'ele-hā-o-Puna and some of the Ulu soldiers were set on one side of the canoe; Ka-lau-meki and the rest of the Ulu men were on the other. Kawelo, Ka-malama, and Kāne-wahine-iki-aoha placed themselves in the middle. The battle that followed was fierce, and so much sand and dust were kicked up that it was difficult to see what was happening. The Ulu men found themselves isolated and thought the war was being lost. They retreated to the canoe and told Kawelo that his foster sons and brother were dead. Then the dust lifted and Kawelo saw this was not so. In fact,

Ka-malama had captured Kū-ahi-lau and was bringing him as prisoner. Kawelo swung his war club and Kū-ahi-lau fell dead.

Then Kawelo scolded the Ulu and told them that if he won
Kaua'i, they would have no part of the victory. They would be
remembered for their cowardice alone.

There was a brief moment of rest before a new onslaught came
marching down the hill. Two more of 'Aikanaka's generals, Wala-
he'e-i-kio and Maumau-i-kio, challenged the invaders. In this melee,
Ka-'ele-hā-o-Puna was wounded on the hand and withdrew from
battle. Ka-malama and Ka-lau-meki continued on, although they
were very tired and their reflexes were noticeably slower. Then
Kawelo challenged Maumau-i-kio to a duel, taunting him to throw
his spear first. Kawelo deflected Maumau-i-kio's spear with a flap of
his *malo,* while Ka-malama grabbed Wala-he'e-i-kio's spear out of
the air with one hand. The two men, filled with shame, turned to
run but they were struck down with their own spears.

Once again 'Aikanaka's messenger appeared before him nude
and with a new bloody scratch on his back. 'Aikanaka said, "Now
my bones feel cold. The rafters that gave us shelter are broken."

The warrior Ka-haka-loa stood up then. "Kawelo learned the
strokes of the war club from his father-in-law, Kalona-i-ka-hai-
lā'au. Even so, we have nothing to fear, for I, too, was taught by
Kalona-i-ka-hai-lā'au. I know all the strokes Kawelo knows. He
cannot kill me."

Ka-haka-loa, after his boasts that he would overcome Kawelo,
strode off down the hill to challenge Kawelo. He immediately ran
into a barrage of insults, a favorite ploy of those days to enrage an
opponent, for an angry foe is more apt to make mistakes than one
who is calm. Kawelo compared *"haka,"* meaning "chief" with *"haka,"*
meaning a shelf, which had the desired effect of angering Ka-
haka-loa.

During the ensuing battle, Kawelo managed to cut off one of Ka-
haka-loa's little toes, a little finger, and the tip of one ear. Then Ka-
haka-loa swung his war club sideways and hit Kawelo in the stomach. Kawelo fell to the ground and lay there.

Ka-haka-loa boasted: "Kawelo is dead!"

Ka-'ehu-iki-'awa-kea, having learned to be suspicious this day,
suggested that Ka-haka-loa hit Kawelo again to make sure he was
dead. "I see his eyes still looking at us," he said.

Ka-haka-loa answered: "If he rises again, then truly he is a god, for the man whom I have struck once never rises again." And he chanted his reason.

Ua make he laau na ka ui,	He is dead, for it is the blow from the young,
Hookahi no laau a ka ui make,	The young makes but one blow to kill,
O iho auanei a hiki i lalo i o Milu	Else he will go down to Milu
I aku i hahau alua ia e Ka-haka-loa.	And say that he was struck twice by Ka-haka-loa.

Ka-'ehu-iki-'awa-kea was not in a position to argue and went back up Nounou with Ka-haka-loa. Here 'Aikanaka ordered his steward to prepared a symbolic meal for his victorious general. A chicken was killed, for was Kawelo not compared to a *moa*, a wild chicken? The bird was wrapped in *ti* leaves and cooked in a calabash filled with hot stones. While Ka-haka-loa ate, 'Aikanaka asked about his missing toe, finger, and ear, but Ka-haka-loa dismissed their loss, saying they stuck out and so were expendable. When he was through eating, Ka-haka-loa placed his empty *poi* calabash over his head, because he did not wish to wear his feathered helmet for it was decorated with rooster feathers. Then he took up his war club and went down to get Kawelo's body so it could be offered as a sacrifice.

Kawelo, however, was not dead. He had been winded when the war club struck his solar plexus with such force but, under the care of Ka-malama and Kāne-wahine-iki-aoha, he quickly recovered and was waiting for Ka-haka-loa.

As Ka-haka-loa approached, Kawelo hurled more insults. "*Lae pa'a*, branded son of a slave! *'Ai lōpāpā*, eater of rubbish! Dog! *'Ai heu*, eater of other men's leavings!" Ka-haka-loa was stunned.

Kawelo tapped him on the top of the calabash he was wearing, forcing it down over his eyes. Before Ka-haka-loa could get his eyes clear, Kawelo raised his club and smashed the calabash into pieces. Kawelo crowed his war cry once again.

When Ka-'ehu-iki-'awa-kea returned to 'Aikanaka with this news, 'Aikanaka realized why Ka-haka-loa had been maimed. He had been cut in the same manner that pigs are cut to mark them as belonging to the chief. "How could he have lived, for he was only Kawelo's pig."

"Summon Ka-uahoa," 'Aikanaka told Ka-'ehu-iki-'awa-kea. "We have no hope left except him. Only he can beat Kawelo."

Kawelo saw Ka-uahoa coming down the hill with his war club, which was a branch torn from the fabulous trunkless koa tree of Ka-hiki-kolo, the same tree that had furnished Kamapua'a's war club a few centuries earlier. Ka-uahoa was a formidable sight. He was easily twice the size of Kawelo and well educated in the strokes of a war club. A blow from him would indeed be fatal. For the first time Kawelo wondered if he had met his match. But he had never backed away from any contest with Ka-uahoa. He had beaten him once and could again. Kawelo picked up his club and took his stand. Kāne-wahine-iki-aoha stood just behind him on his right and Ka-malama took up a position on the left. Ka-lau-meki and Ka-'ele-hā-o-Puna stood behind him.

Waiting for his opponent to arrive and take up his position, Kawelo remembered the incident in their youth when Kawelo had deliberately broken Ka-uahoa's kite, and Ka-uahoa had not retaliated. Gradually, Kawelo began to take pity on his opponent, remembering their childhood days. He composed and chanted a *paha*:

E kapae ke kaua, e ka hoahanau!	Turn aside from war, o brother!
E waiho la oe i'au i kou hoahanau!	Let me, your brother, alone!
Aole hoi i na la o kuu hoike,	This is not the day for me to reveal to
kuu pili makamaka!	you my close kinship,
Ku'u hoa kolohe o ka wa kamalii,	My mischievous companion in childhood days,
Hoa kui lei lehua o Waikae — e —!	My companion who strung lehua flower garlands at Waikae!
Lehua a kaua e kui kane ai,	The lehua blossoms that we strung in our boyhood,
Me na kaikuana haku o kaua!	With our royal elder brothers!

To this, Ka-uahoa answered: "The time to remember our childhood is gone. Today we will give battle. Today either my club will seek your death or your club will seek mine. Today on one of us must fall the heavy sickness."

Ka-uahoa lifted his war club. Immediately Kāne-wahine-iki-aoha threw her *pikoi*, which became entangled in the branches of Ka-uahoa's war club, and she deflected his downward blow. As Ka-uahoa began to straighten up again, Kawelo raised his club, swung mightily, and almost cut Ka-uahoa in two. The final contest between these birth-brothers was as short as it was brutal.

Now only 'Aikanaka was left. Kawelo and Kāne-wahine-iki-aoha climbed Nounou. 'Aikanaka thought he should go to meet Kawelo, but his priests said, "How can you go to meet Kawelo, for you are a king and he is a servant. His grandfather was nothing but a counter of cockroaches who lived in the uplands of Kula-huhu, Nā-hana-i-moa by name." This had been said loud enough for the approaching warrior to hear.

This remark filled Kawelo with great shame, for he thought his wife would be ashamed of him for being called a born servant. He was about to jump over the cliff when Kāne-wahine-iki-aoha threw her *pikoi* again and caught him. "How strange of you!" she scolded. "If you really were a born slave, you would have been killed during the battle. You are a rooster, and roosters sleep on top of the house of kings. Tell 'Aikanaka that."

He 'lii ka moa,	The chicken is the king,
Kau ana ka moa i luna o ka hale,	The chicken roosts on the house,
A hiia ko poo e Aikanaka.	And sits covering your head, Aikanaka.
O ka moa kou mea e ala ai,	The chicken wakes you up in the morning,
He 'lii ka moa e, he 'lii.	The chicken is a king, it is a king.

'Aikanaka, at the advice of his priests, replied, "Chickens are servants." This time Kawelo was ready.

Haku ia nae hoi ka hulu o ka moa,	The feathers of the chickens are plaited,
I kahili i mua o na 'lii.	Into kahili that stand in the presence of kings.
Kahili ia nae hoi ko kua e Aikanaka.	Your back, Aikanaka, is brushed by the kahili.
Nolaila, he 'lii ka moa.	Therefore chickens are kings.
He lii ka moa e Aikanaka,	Chickens are kings, Aikanaka,
Aohe kauwa e.	And not servants.

There was no further sound from 'Aikanaka. When Kawelo and Kāne-wahine-iki-aoha at last entered the *heiau,* it was empty. 'Aikanaka had fled. His army lay dead on the plains below, and he was never one to enjoy face-to-face combat. Kaua'i belonged to Kawelo. His parents were avenged.

Kawelo gave the district of Halele'a to his wife, Kāne-wahine-iki-aoha; Ko'olau went to Ka-lau-meki; Ka-'ele-hā-o-Puna stayed with

Kawelo to manage Puna; and Ka-malama took over the Kona district. Peace descended on Kaua'i once again.

Not for long, however. Ka-'ele-hā-o-Puna awoke one morning with the desire to visit the Mānā lands and started off. As evening fell, he arrived at Wahiawa and was invited to spend the night. His host had another guest, none other than 'Aikanaka himself. After leaving Nounou, 'Aikanaka had gone into hiding in Kō'ula valley. From time to time he would come down to the shore of Wahiawa. He immediately recognized Ka-'ele-hā-o-Puna and sat the youngster down, fed him, and invited him to spend the night in the company of his daughter Kawelo-'eha.

Ka-'ele-hā-o-Puna fell in love with Kawelo-'eha, and the two were quickly married. This led to a problem for Ka-'ele-hā-o-Puna's sense of honor. He had little to give in return for 'Ai-kanaka's kindness to him. He thought hard about this and his wife kept reminding him of his obligation. At last Ka-'ele-hā-o-Puna offered 'Aikanaka a gift beyond price, the information that Kawelo had never learned to defend himself against an attack by stones. Stones could be thrown by hand, and experts with the sling could fell an opponent at a distance with a well-placed throw. 'Aikanaka immediately sought out his still loyal followers and began to collect piles of rocks of all sizes. Huge cairns were raised on the plains of Wahiawa.

Rumors of this activity reached Kawelo in Wailua and he sent a messenger asking Ka-malama in Waimea to investigate. Ka-malama did so, and in a brief talk with Ka-'ele-hā-o-Puna realized his betrayal of Kawelo's secret. Ka-malama turned to head for Kawelo to report, but Ka-'ele-hā-o-Puna attacked him. In a fierce battle, these men and their followers fought and Ka-malama fell back to Koloa hoping to find a canoe. While Ka-malama was defending himself from attack coming from his front, Ka-'ele-hā-o-Puna stabbed him in the back with his spear and Ka-malama fell dead.

When Kawelo heard this, he immediately headed for Wahiawa, sending messages to his wife, Kāne-wahine-iki-aoha, and foster son Ka-lau-meki. Kawelo did not wait for these two and arrived at Wahiawa alone to find 'Aikanaka and Ka-'ele-hā-o-Puna waiting for him. Kawelo was stoned and, ignorant of this method of warfare, could do nothing to defend himself. Three times he was covered with stones, three times he recovered. After the fourth time, 'Aikanaka found Kawelo's body bruised, battered, and to all appearances dead.

'Aikanaka ordered the body wrapped in strips of banana stalks and carried to the Maulili *heiau* in Koloa. There Kawelo was laid on the altar to be offered as a sacrifice the following morning. The guardians of the *heiau* were Kawelo's sister and her husband. During the night they heard a groan from the altar, found Kawelo barely conscious and, with massage, a little food, and much care, helped him recover his strength.

In the morning when 'Aikanaka and his men returned to the *heiau*, they were met with a revived Kawelo who, with his war club Ku'ika'a, killed the astonished 'Aikanaka and many of his men before they could defend themselves. Only Ka-'ele-hā-o-Puna was spared, for Kawelo considered him his son.

Meanwhile Kāne-wahine-iki-aoha and Ka-lau-meki had gathered soldiers and followed Kawelo. As their canoes arrived at Koloa, they saw many soldiers running hither and thither, and as soon as they learned these were followers of 'Aikanaka began slaughtering as many as they could. They found the body of Ka-malama and brought it with them to Maulili where Kawelo was.

Kāne-wahine-iki-aoha and Ka-lau-meki demanded that Kawelo put Ka-'ele-hā-o-Puna to death for his treachery, but Kawelo could not bring himself to kill his foster son. Then Kāne-wahine-iki-aoha laid Ka-malama's body at Kawelo's feet, face down, showing the fatal wound in his back.

Kawelo led Ka-'ele-hā-o-Puna out of the *heiau* and with one blow of Ku'ika'a killed him. Ka-malama was his true brother, son of the parents whose honor he had avenged by coming back to Kaua'i to fight a war against 'Aikanaka. Ka-'ele-hā-o-Puna had denied Ka-malama the death of a warrior fighting face to face against his foes by stabbing him in the back. Yet Kawelo loved both of them. He could only express his sorrow in his last chant:

Hilihili ula, hilihili lei,	Red streaks, wreathed streaks,
Pali koekoe i ka hoa olelo ole	Cold are the companionless hills
I momoe ai kaua, e kuu kana!	Where we slept, O my son!
He kiu leho—puu ka makani,	A watchful humped cowrie is the wind,
Leho helehelei ia ia li,	A shell tossed about by the chief,
Haukeke make i ke anu,	Shivering to death with the cold,
Ona heu la, e	The bristling cold,
He anu!	The cold!
He anu alana ana i kai,	The cold breeze wafted to the sea,
Ka mokumoku, ka hookui,	A cutting cold, the chill of death,

Ka luna i pueo ana-alia!	Up to the cave of the owl there await!
Piha mai luna o Aahoaka	Filled are the uplands of Aahoaka
I ko paa kaua!	With your war garment!
He paa kaua au na a'aua a moa,	I am skilled at war like a tough old rooster,
Ua pii kakala, akaakaa ka hulu!	Whose spurs stick out, bristling with rage!
Ke kau ana oia Moa la!	Here stands Rooster!
Mahi ia Moa!	Strong is Rooster!

At this moment, the legends stop. Kawelo, some say, lived a long life. Others, perhaps more correctly, hint that Kawelo became so obsessed with killing 'Aikanaka's wife and children that he demanded he be carried from place to place to search frantically for them, no matter the time of day or the danger to his carriers. Eventually, fearing for their own lives, his followers threw him over a cliff into the Hanapēpē valley.

In any event, not much time passed between the death of 'Aikanaka and the time Kū-ali'i arrived as *ali'i nui* of Kaua'i. The direct line of ruling chiefs, from eldest son to eldest son that had begun with Ahukini-a-La'a twelve generations before had been broken.

6

MUKU
The End

DREAMS OF CONQUEST NOW SWEPT OVER KAUAʻI, LEAVING ONLY ruin in their wake. Under Kū-aliʻi, Kauaʻi supplied men and arms to the wars that spread over the windward islands as Kū-aliʻi and his son Pele-i-ʻō-hōlani established a multi-island kingdom. Kahekili of Maui also dreamed of unifying all the islands into one kingdom. During a century of constant warfare, countless members of the *aliʻi* class died until by 1824 only the Kamehameha family and their hangers-on claimed *aliʻi* status.

Niʻaupiʻo births continued until there were great numbers of them, all surrounded by the most stringent *kapu*. Infractions meant death. The *kānāwai* spoke of punishment for lawbreakers; few spoke of the welfare of the people.

In 1778, Western civilization, in the form of Captain James Cook, captain of the *Discovery*, reached these islands. This Englishman's ship was filled with iron, something the natives had seldom seen, yet they immediately realized the value of a steel blade over a wooden one. As parting gifts, Captain Cook left behind fleas and the venereal disease syphilis.

Captain Cook was followed by Yankee whalers out from New England to catch whales in Alaskan waters and render them into oil for lighting. These Yankees quickly discovered that it was better to winter in Hawai'i while merchantmen ships, more suited for tran-shipping tuns of whale oil, carried the produce home. These mer-chantmen returned to Hawai'i during the summer when it was eas-ier to round Cape Horn. While waiting for summer to end and the whalers to return to Hawai'i, these merchantmen found that the islands had forests of sandalwood. They gleefully bought the fragrant wood cheaply from the naive inhabitants and took it to China, where they sold the wood for an immense profit.

The native inhabitants of these isolated islands were over-whelmed. They were introduced to new technologies and new con-cepts: cloth that was more durable than *kapa*, guns that were more efficient in killing than their own wooden weapons, and the star-tling realization that the sailors freely broke all the *kapu* and no heavenly retribution fell on them.

In 1819, after Kamehameha died, his widows Ka-'ahu-manu and Ke-ōpū-o-lani ate a meal with his son and heir Liholiho. This had been forbidden since the time when Wākea, the Sky Father, had lusted after his daughter. This one act destroyed the ancient *kapu* system. The old gods no longer walked the earth and no longer cared for their people.

Diseases against which the Hawaiians had no immunity proved fatal. Cholera, typhus, mumps, measles, smallpox, venereal diseases, and leprosy all took terrible tolls.

Six months after Liholiho and Ka-'ahu-manu's fateful meal, Congregational missionaries from New England arrived with several Hawaiian men on board who had been abandoned far from their homeland. The Congregationalists had educated them and been persuaded by them to sail to Hawai'i to bring the gospel to their peo-ple. The missionaries found a familiar adversary, the godless Yankee sailor, and heard the welcome news that the ancient Hawaiian reli-gion had already been abolished. The missionaries spoke of their one God and created an alphabet for the Hawaiian language so that con-verts could read the Bible for themselves. These waves of influence, of cultures and disease, and the dreams of conquest by successive chiefs of the windward islands destroyed much of the ancient Hawaiian civilization. The last five generations of Polynesian rule on Kaua'i, beginning with Kū-ali'i, led their people through these perilous times. The *pua ali'i* found that the forces arrayed against them were too strong, too bewildering. It is no wonder the Kū-ali'i family was considered a doomed race.

Kū-aliʻi

In order to obtain a handful of warriors and a double canoe, Kawelo-lei-makua agreed to cede Kauaʻi to Kū-aliʻi in case both Kawelo and his enemy ʻAikanaka died as a result of the coming war. To Kū-aliʻi, who had been fighting to possess Oʻahu and had now extended his field of operations to conquering Maui, this double death was a possibility.

In any case, he had as good a claim to Kauaʻi as any other living *aliʻi.*

His grandmother was Kawelo-lau-huki, daughter of Kawelo-mahamaha-iʻa. He had inherited the *kumukānāwai* of his great-grandmother Ka-hā-malu-ʻihi (frequently known as Ka-lua-o-Hoʻo-hila in chants), she who had been wife both to Kā-kuhi-hewa and his son Kāne-kapu-a-Kā-kuhi-hewa. He had also been to Kauaʻi once as a young man to gather *kauila* wood for the weapons he needed for his warriors. He also made a war club of *kauila,* which he called Huli-moku-alana *(Victorious land turning).* At that time Kawelo-lei-makua had been his guide.

Kū-aliʻi's *kānāwai* was called Niʻaupiʻo Kolowalu. It said that old men and women could sleep safely along the highways without being molested in any way. It also said that farmers and fishermen had to welcome strangers and feed the hungry. If a man said he was hungry, he must be fed if he invoked this law. Once the *kānāwai* had been invoked, the food became dedicated to the gods and to this use only. Failure to feed the hungry man then resulted in the death of the owner of the food. If a man had invoked the law with the intent to rob another of his food and provisions, however, then the penalty of death fell on him, not on his unwilling host.

When he heard that Kawelo had killed ʻAikanaka and that Kawelo's subjects had thrown him over a cliff, Kū-aliʻi hurried to Kauaʻi and declared himself *aliʻi nui.* He installed his son Pele-iʻō-hōlani as governor, reporting only to Kū-aliʻi himself. Kū-aliʻi by this time was already the ruler of a united Oʻahu after several successful battles. He assessed Kauaʻi for its ability to produce raw materials and men for his army. He was pleased with what he saw and immediately returned to Oʻahu. Assisted by fresh weapons and men, he turned his attention to Molokaʻi, Lānaʻi, and Maui and soon had installed himself as *aliʻi nui* of these islands.

Kū-aliʻi lived to a very great old age and is said to have been carried into his last battle in a hammock slung from the shoulders of two warriors.

At his death, his oldest son, Ka-pi'o-ho'okā-lani, inherited the island of O'ahu. Pele-i'ō-hōlani remained on Kaua'i.

Pele-i'ō-hōlani

Not long after he had become the governor of Kaua'i, Pele-i'ō-hō-lani quarreled with his father, Kū-ali'i, while visiting him on O'ahu. The quarrel grew until Pele-i'ō-hōlani dared to attack his father physically. In the resulting scuffle, Kū-ali'i caught his son in a *lua* hold and hoisted him over his head. *Lua* was a deadly martial art, one that took years of training, and was designed to break an opponent's bones, permanently crippling him, or to kill him, usually by swinging the victim down over one's raised knee, breaking his back. Kū-ali'i was old and his strength was unexpected. For a breathless moment Pele-i'ō-hōlani knew his father could kill him easily. Kū-ali'i, having made his point, released his son. Pele-i'ō-hōlani returned to Kaua'i and never again defied his father.

Although war had not yet come to Kaua'i, there was uneasiness, for outside events were crashing in on this peaceful society. Then to everyone's surprise a small fleet of double canoes arrived off shore. Its passengers, men, women, and children, were starving, and from the appearance of the canoes it seemed they had gone through a strong storm. These newcomers were somewhat darker than the local people, and their leader, Kokoa, was tattooed with representations of birds, sharks, and other fishes. These people knew how to grow taro and were familiar with all the arts and crafts of the local society. The local chief, whose name is not given in the legend, gave Kokoa and his people land within the Waimea canyon complex. There they settled down.

In a short while, the local people noticed that these newcomers were not following the *kapu*. Their women were eating bananas, coconuts and all sorts of fish as well as pork, which were strictly forbidden to the old-time residents. The people protested, and their *konohiki* chief went to Kokoa to ask him to obey the local customs. For a time Kokoa and his people followed the *kapu* but soon reverted to their own customs. The *konohiki* objected again but this time caught sight of Kokoa's daughter Palua, a very beautiful woman. The *konohiki* fell in love and proposed. Even after her marriage, Palua refused to pay attention to the *kapu* and openly flaunted her ways. The *kahuna* of Waimea was outraged and demanded that Palua be put to death. The *konohiki* wanted instead to return Palua to her father, but the *kahuna* insisted. Palua was strangled, and her body thrown into the sea.

Kokoa, in return, killed one of the *konohiki*'s relatives, and he and his followers feasted on the body. They were cannibals and therefore obviously not descended from Hawai'i-loa and his *kānāwai* Papa-enaena forbidding such a revolting deed. Kokoa led his people away from his enraged neighbors and fled to Hā'upu mountain for a time until their cannibalism became known to their neighbors. In the night, Kokoa led his people over the ridge to Koloa, where they stole some canoes and sailed to O'ahu.

Word eventually came back that the cannibals had been killed, but nonetheless there was a greater sense of uneasiness than ever. Such an event seemed an omen of future troubles.

Then Kū-ali'i died. His oldest son, Ka-pi'o-ho'okā-lani, became ruler of O'ahu. He immediately raised an army and invaded Molo-ka'i. His timing was unfortunate. A chief of Hawai'i, Alapa'i-nui, had invaded Maui to find that its chief Kekaulike had just died. Ala-pa'i-nui's own sister Ke-ku'i-apo-iwa and his nephew Kamehameha-nui were now joint rulers. The reason for war was over, and Alapa'i-nui was relaxing before returning to Hawai'i. As soon as he heard the news that Moloka'i, always an appendage of Maui, had been invaded, Alapa'i-nui gathered his army and went to Moloka'i. After five days of fierce battle, Ka-pi'o-ho'okā-lani was killed and his army routed back to O'ahu.

Alapa'i-nui followed them and landed at Kailua, in the district of Ko'olaupoko. For a month, there were skirmishes, for neither side could launch a major offensive. Meanwhile, Ka-naha-o-ka-lani, who had succeeded his father, Ka-pi'o-ho'okā-lani, as ruling chief of O'ahu, sent a message to his uncle Pele-i'ō-hōlani to come to his assistance.

Pele-i'ō-hōlani went aboard his war canoe, Kāne-'ai'ai, and sailed to Wai'anae on O'ahu. Immediately the Wai'anae chief Nā-'ili set off for Alapa'i-nui to arrange a peace settlement. As it happened, one of the chiefs in Alapa'i-nui's group was Ka-lani-'ōpu'u. Ka-lani-'ōpu'u and his half-brother Keōua led Nā-'ili to Alapa'i-nui. There it was decided that Alapa'i-nui and Pele-i'ō-hōlani would meet face to face, completely alone and unarmed, to determine the fate of the war. They met, and the end result was that Alapaʻi-nui returned to Hawaiʻi.

On Maui, Ka-uhi-ʻai-moku-a-Kama, brother of Kamehameha-nui, rebelled. Alapaʻi-nui returned and Ka-uhi-ʻai-moku-a-Kama asked Pele-i-ʻō-hōlani to help him. The battle raged for a few days and ended only when once again Alapaʻi-nui and Pele-i-ʻō-hōlani met face to face and both agreed to sail home. Ka-uhi-ʻai-moku-a-Kama, the rebellious brother, had been taken prisoner and drowned by Alapaʻi-nui, and Kamehameha-nui was once again secure as Maui's ruler.

Pele-i-ʻō-hōlani returned to Oʻahu and became *aliʻi nui*. When certain Molokaʻi chiefs killed his daughter Ke-ʻē-lani-honua-iā-kama, Pele-i-ʻō-hōlani descended upon that island. Before he was done, he had either killed, burned, or driven off the island all the *aliʻi* families but one.

Ka-ʻapuwai

When Pele-i-ʻō-hōlani left Kauaʻi to pursue his destiny as the future ruler of the Oʻahu kingdom, he left his daughter Ka-ʻapuwai as governor of Kauaʻi. She was the first chiefess since Ka-ʻili-lau-o-ke-koa, some centuries before, to become the paramount ruler.

She was married to Ka-ʻume-he-iwā, a high chief of Kauaʻi. They were both descended from Ka-lani-kukuma, and their marriage joined the junior and senior genealogical lines that stemmed from their common ancestor, thus giving their daughter Ka-maka-helei a stronger *mana* than either of her parents.

Ka-ʻapuwai died before her father, and the government of Kauaʻi passed to Ka-maka-helei.

Ka-maka-helei

For a time, Ka-maka-helei lived as her ancestors had. She was the *aliʻi wahine nui* of Kauaʻi but fully aware that she owed allegiance to her grandfather Pele-i-ʻō-hōlani.

Her choice of husbands embroiled her in warfare, whether that was her intention or not. Her first husband was a Kauaʻi chief, Kiha, and with him she had three children: first a daughter, Lele-māhoa-lani, then a son, Keawe, and finally another daughter, Ka-lua-i-pihana.

Then Pele-i-ʻō-hōlani sent his grandson Ka-neoneo to Kauaʻi to ensure that the island would remain loyal to him. Ka-neoneo and Ka-maka-helei were first cousins, and soon Ka-maka-helei put Kiha aside and took Ka-neoneo for her husband.

Kiha fled to Ni'ihau and gathered a small number of warriors about him. He led raids to the south coast of Kaua'i against the forces of Ka-neoneo. In one such raid, Kiha himself was killed. Peace, such as it was, settled over the people of Kaua'i for a short time.

On O'ahu, Kūmahana, who was Pele-i'ō-hōlani's regent, proved himself to be an entirely unsatisfactory ruler. The O'ahu chiefs rebelled against him and sent Kūmahana, his wives, and children into exile on Kaua'i. Pele-i'ō-hōlani returned posthaste from his skirmishes against Kahekili on Maui to renew his claim to O'ahu.

Kahekili, the highest ranking chief on Maui, took this opportunity to lead his forces once again against those of Pele-i'ō-hōlani. After several battles, Kahekili was victorious. To consolidate his rule, he married his sister Kalola to Ka-lani-'ōpu'u of Hawai'i in the hopes that he would either help by sending men and arms or, at least, remain indifferent to the situation. This was part of a long-term plan, for within Kahekili burned the ambition to become the first ruler of the entire Hawaiian archipelago.

From O'ahu, Pele-i'ō-hōlani sent for Ka-neoneo to join him to help stem Kahekili's ambition.

This left Ka-maka-helei vulnerable. Although she was the nominal ruler of Kaua'i, her uncle Kūmahana began to make moves to take over the government. Kahekili of Maui was quick to realize the opportunity this presented to neutralize Kaua'i. He sent his young half-brother Ka-'eo-kū-lani to Kaua'i to woo Ka-maka-helei.

Ka-'eo-kū-lani was successful. His presence made Kūmahana's threat less potent. Since she was nine years older than Ka-'eo-kū-lani, she did not expect to bear any more children, and her oldest son, Keawe, was named heir to the kingdom.

For the first time in centuries, every island was involved in one man's dream of conquest. At the end of 1777, Ka-lani-'ōpu'u was slowly but surely winning his way to become the paramount chief of Hawai'i. A young chief in his court named Kamehameha burned with the same dream of conquest.

By this time, all of Maui, Moloka'i, and Lāna'i were under the rule of Kahekili who had succeeded in taking them from Pele-i'ō-hōlani. He was gearing up for an invasion of O'ahu where Pele-i'ō-hōlani, now a very old man, had turned over the government to his grand-son Ka-neoneo.

On Kaua'i, Ka-maka-helei must have had torn loyalties. Her grandfather was Pele-i'ō-hōlani, Ka-neoneo was the father of her daughter Ka-pua'a-moku. Her new husband, Ka-'eo-kū-lani, was fiercely loyal to his older brother, Kahekili.

Even the blindest *kilokilo*, predictors of the future, could discern much bloodshed to come.

Into this volatile, war-filled moment, Captain James Cook arrived. In the late afternoon of of January 19, 1778, Captain Cook, commander of the ship *Discovery*, saw the island of O'ahu in the distance. Tides and wind being against him, he beat to the west and at sunset saw Kaua'i in the distance. He determined to land there to replenish his ship with food and water.

That night, off Koloa, Moapu, a fisherman, and his companions were trolling the deep-sea grounds with heavy lines. A strange thing, something completely new to them, passed them. There were small fires on board this object, which was a different shape than any dou-ble canoe. Moapu and his friends dropped their lines and hurried ashore to tell Ka-'eo-kū-lani and Ka-maka-helei of this apparition that clearly frightened them.

The next morning, the strange object lay outside Ka'ahe at Wai-mea. Those who saw it understood that it was a ship they were look-ing at, with tall masts and sails shaped like a giant *hīhīmanu* (manta ray). Some spectators were terrified. Their first thought was that the god Lono, as he had promised, was returning on a floating island. Everyone was excited, and Waimea echoed with their shouts and exclamations.

The *kahuna nui*, Kū-'ohu, declared, "That can be nothing else than the *heiau* of the god Lono. In the center is the tower of the demigod Ke-o-lewa, and there in the back is the place of sacrifice at the altar." Coming from such a reliable source as the chief priest, the rumor grew that the leader of this ship was indeed the god Lono.

Kū-'ohu, however, after several days of close observation, had doubts that this was Lono. He consulted his sacred cup, Ka-ipu-'aumakua, and concluded that these were not gods but men. They were, he said, just like the two white priests who had come to these islands from a foreign country when Paumakua was living, close to a thousand years ago. They were like the *haole* Kū-ali'i had seen on his travels less than a hundred years earlier.

But, until they were absolutely sure, it was safer to be prudent. Ka-maka-helei hurriedly called a conference of chiefs. She said, "Let us not fight against our god. Let us please him that he may be favorable to us."

She sent three men on board to see what this strange ship really was and to assess those on board. These three were the *kahuna* Kū'ohu, wearing his *lei palaoa* (necklace of woven human hair holding a hook of carved whale ivory), chief Kāne-a-ka-ho'owaha, and chief Ki'i-kīkī who was Ka-'eo-kū-lani's trusted man who had come with him from Maui.

As they neared the *Discovery*, they saw an extraordinary amount of iron. Iron had come to the islands a few times in the past in the form of nails in boards from shipwrecks. The three went on board and saw many men with white foreheads, wrinkled skins, and angular heads. They spoke a strange language, and most impressive of all, they breathed fire from their mouths.

Ki'i-kīkī and Kū'ohu recognized Captain Cook as the leader of these men. They bowed to him, murmured a prayer, and then, each taking one of Cook's hands, they knelt down.

Captain Cook gave Kū'ohu a dagger, a gift beyond price. It was the first gift from Western civilization to Hawai'i, and it was considered an omen. Ki'i-kīkī, a trained soldier, immediately recognized that owning iron weapons would give him and his ruling chief an advantage over others.

Returning to shore, Ki'i-kīkī reported to Ka-'eo-kū-lani and described the dagger. Ka-pupu'u, one of the guards surrounding Ka-'eo-kū-lani, immediately said, "I will go on board and take some iron for us."

Ka-'eo-kū-lani replied, "No. Kū-'ohu has warned us not to take the god's property, so that there will be no trouble between him and us."

Ka-pupu'u, remembering legends of skilled thieves who became rich and honored in their lifetimes, did not listen. He went out to the ship and saw quantities of iron things just lying about on deck. He grabbed as many pieces as he could and threw them into his canoe. One of the ship's guards raised his rifle and shot Ka-pupu'u dead. He was the first Hawaiian to die by a bullet.

No Hawaiian knew what to make of this strange thing that could kill from a distance. For a time, they thought it was the noise that killed and named guns after the only things they knew that spouted

96 in the same way: Wai-kī (*Water-squirter*) and Wai-pahu (*Water-gusher*).

Some chiefs thought that Captain Cook should be put to death for killing Ka-pupuʻu but the *kahuna* Kūʻohu said, "No, they were not to blame for that. Ka-pupuʻu was to blame, for he went to steal even though our *aliʻi nui* had forbidden it."

The following day, Captain Cook came ashore for the first time. His longboat landed at the mouth of the Waimea river, on the beach of Luhi beside Lāʻau-ʻōkala point. He was greeted by a huge crowd of people pushing and shoving to get a look at this, as many thought, living god come among them. People had come from Nāpali, Mānā, and Kīpū like a rushing stream during the night.

Captain Cook wandered about Waimea for a time before returning to his ship. *Kahuna* Kū-ʻohu suggested, "I do not know if these are men or gods. Let us offer them our women. If they are gods, they will refuse the gift. If they are men, they will accept them."

Ka-maka-helei presented gifts to Cook: hogs, chickens, bananas, taro, sweet potatoes, sugarcane, yams, fine mats, and tapa cloth. In return Cook presented them with cloth, iron, a sword, knives, bead necklaces, and mirrors.

Then Ka-maka-helei offered Cook her own daughter, Lele-mahoe-lani. According to the Kauaʻi source of this story, she spent the night on board with Cook. She left the following morning laden with presents.

When other women saw that a high chiefess had slept on board with Captain Cook himself (although in the official records this was denied), they, too, went with the officers and sailors and in this way obtained lengths of cloth, bits of iron, and mirrors for themselves.

A few days later, his ship loaded with water and fresh food, Captain Cook left Waimea. He left behind a puzzled and frightened population still not sure whether he was a man or a god.

Ka-ʻeo-kū-lani quickly understood the superiority that rifles and guns would give him. He also appreciated the fact that some of the people on board the ships that followed close on the heels of Captain Cook had knowledge that would be immensely valuable. Among these was a gunner and ship's armorer named, in Hawaiian, Mare Amara, who left his ship to join Ka-ʻeo-kū-lani.

In 1780, Ka-maka-helei gave birth to another son, Ka-umu-aliʻi.

The situation on Maui grew uncomfortable for Kahekili. He sent a message to his brother Ka-ʻeo-kū-lani to return to Maui. Ka-ʻeo-kū-lani brought his two trusted counselors, Ki'i-kīkī and Kai-'awa, with him. Ka-umu-ali'i, his son with Ka-maka-helei, was declared heir to Kaua'i, passing over his older half-brother, Keawe. Since Ka-umu-ali'i was still a child, he and his government were put in the hands of Inamo'o as regent.

Inamo'o was unpopular, and some chiefs rebelled after a time. Inamo'o put them down ruthlessly and shipped off some prisoners with the news to Ka-'eo-kū-lani. It was Kahekili, on O'ahu, who responded and made a lightning trip to Kaua'i to assess the situation for himself. He left Inamo'o as regent and returned to O'ahu a sick man. He died in the autumn of 1793.

The island of O'ahu now fell to Kahekili's son Ka-lani-kū-pule, aided by his brother Koa-lau-kani. Ka-'eo-kū-lani laid claim to Maui, Moloka'i, and Lāna'i. After a year of peace, Ka-'eo-kū-lani grew homesick for Kaua'i. He sailed with a large fleet of canoes to Moloka'i and then on to Waimānalo on O'ahu.

Unfortunately, Ka-lani-kū-pule thought that Ka-'eo-kū-lani was coming to invade him, and a furious battle was fought as the Maui troops attempted to come ashore. The leader of the O'ahu army was shot by Mare Amara, Ka-'eo-kū-lani's gunner, as he stood at the ramparts wearing his red feather cloak, a highly visible object.

For two days and nights Ka-'eo-kū-lani kept his fleet offshore, sending messengers to ask for a meeting. Finally the two chiefs met. Ka-lani-kū-pule called off the battle, and the two chiefs mourned the newly dead as well as the death of Kahekili.

Ka-'eo-kū-lani took his fleet to Wai'anae on the southwest corner of O'ahu to prepare for the trip across the notoriously dangerous Ka'ie'iewaho channel to Kaua'i. There he discovered that his two counselors, Ki'i-kīkī and Kai-'awa, were planning to throw him overboard in mid channel, return the fleet to O'ahu, and conquer it.

Ka-'eo-kū-lani quickly decided that he preferred to die in battle amongst many than to die a lonely death at sea. He ordered his canoes dismantled and made preparations to march on Ka-lani-kū-pule. Several battles took place on the 'Ewa plains, which Ka-'eo-kū-lani won easily. Then two foreign ships sailed into Pearl Harbor. Ka-lani-kū-pule managed to hire them soon after their arrival in Hawai'i. The ships were under the command of a certain Captain Brown.

On December 12, 1794, the battle known as Lū-ki'i-'ahu took place. Ka-'eo-kū-lani's troops were on the flats of 'Aiea. The right wing of the Oʻahu army was led by Koa-lau-kani while the shoreline was held by Ka-mohomoho aided by the foreign ships. Ka-lani-kū-pule himself led the center. The Oʻahu forces managed to surround Ka-ʻeo-kū-lani but he fought back hard. The guns from the ship fired into his forces, and Mare Amara attempted to return the fire, hoping to disable one of the ships. Ka-ʻeo-kū-lani and six of his advisors ducked down a ravine, where they were out of sight of the land forces. Unfortunately, Ka-ʻeo-kū-lani's red feather cloak was highly visible to the ships, and they fired round after round into the ravine. Ka-ʻeo-kū-lani was killed.

After the battle, Ka-lani-kū-pule found many of Ka-ʻeo-kū-lani's top chiefs and his wives and executed them. Only Kiʻi-kīkī and Kai-ʻawa, whose treachery had promoted this battle, escaped to Kauaʻi.

Ka-lani-kū-pule had little time to rejoice in his victory. Kame-hameha, chief of Hawaiʻi, had by this time united that island under his rule. He invaded Maui and paused for a moment on Molokaʻi before sweeping the Oʻahu forces over the Nuʻuanu *pali* in 1795. Ka-lani-kū-pule ended as a sacrifice to Kamehameha's blood-thirsty war god.

Next Kamehameha sailed for Kauaʻi but his fleet was destroyed in mid channel by a storm. Kauaʻi breathed a collective sigh of relief. The promise made to Kūkona that never again would any descendant of the Hua chiefs of the windward islands invade Kauaʻi was holding. Kamehameha had broken that promise, and look at what happened to him, came the whispers.

Kamehameha, his fleet damaged, his soldiers demoralized, was nonetheless still determined to bring Kauaʻi into his kingdom. A revolt broke out on Hawaiʻi, however, and Kamehameha quickly returned. He remained there for six years.

Kauaʻi desperately needed that time. It was in political turmoil. Ka-umu-aliʻi had been made heir to the kingdom and was now sixteen years old. Shortly after Kamehameha's attempted invasion, the regent Inamoʻo died, and everyone welcomed the thought that Ka-umu-aliʻi would now take up the kingdom into his own hands.

The records do not indicate what happened to Ka-maka-helei. One source says she became the trusted advisor to her son Ka-umu-aliʻi, but that version offers no explanation why she did not keep the supreme power in her own hands, which she would have had if she were still living.

Keawe

Now Inamo'o died and Ka-maka-helei's oldest son, Keawe, who once had been heir, attacked Wailua and after a brief skirmish captured Ka-umu-ali'i. The young chief became a privileged prisoner, free to wander his lands at Wailua but not to leave unless with Keawe. Keawe declared himself the *ali'i nui*.

Among those who hastened to Keawe's side was Ki'i-kīkī, powerful second-in-command to Ka-'eo-kū-lani, he who had plotted to throw his chief overboard in mid channel. He was the *konohiki* chief of Wainiha *ahupua'a*, and his older brother Kāne-'eku was *konohiki* of Hanapēpē.

For a year, all went well. Keawe had taken possession of all the muskets, guns, and ammunition that had been collected over the years. These now symbolized the power of the *ali'i nui*.

Keawe put his trust in Ki'i-kīkī and Kāne-'eku, for no one had returned from O'ahu to warn him that Ki'i-kīkī was treacherous. The two *konohiki* chiefs persuaded Keawe to tour the island and meet his subjects. They got as far as Kapa'a where Keawe went to bathe in the famous pool Kupa-nihi. While he was bathing, Ki'i-kīkī took up one of the rifles and shot Keawe.

Kāne-'eku advised his brother to return to Wailua at once to kill Ka-umu-ali'i. "Let us pinch off the 'awa leaf bud while the 'awa plant is tender lest its juice become as bitter as gall," he suggested. Ki'i-kīkī refused. He thought he could control the young chief. He took all the guns and went to Polihale while Kāne-'eku returned to Hana-pēpē to await developments.

Ka-umu-ali'i

Ka-umu-ali'i, now freed from Inamo'o's regency and from captivity by his brother Keawe, was acclaimed *ali'i nui* of Kaua'i. He knew he had two very dangerous adversaries who thought they were above his reach. How long before they would shoot him, too, and take over the kingdom? They had in their possession all the guns and ammunition that had been gathered over the years. Ka-umu-ali'i knew he needed an ally, someone more beholden to him than to these powerful chiefs.

Nā-kaikua'ana was a close friend of Ki'i-kīkī and was also a member of Ka-umu-ali'i's court. Claiming deep obligation, Ka-umu-ali'i gave Nā-kaikua'ana permission to sleep with his wives as payment for past favors—all that he had to offer, he claimed. Eagerly Nā-kai-kua'ana did so. After some time had passed, Nā-kaikua'ana realized the consequences of what he was doing. As soon as Ka-umu-ali'i became strong enough, Nā-kaikua'ana's life would be worthless. The other chiefs who served Ka-umu-ali'i, those in charge of his personal property, the *kahili* bearers, and all his kinsmen, would see that he died.

Nā-kaikua'ana went to Ka-umu-ali'i and placed his hands on the young chief's knees. He pledged himself forever to Ka-umu-ali'i and as proof offered a plan to recapture the guns from Ki'i-kīkī.

Ki'i-kīkī was fond of the sport of *he'e nalu* (surfboarding). His favorite place was the surf of Ka-ua, off the coast of Makaweli. Ki'i-kīkī one day went surfing here. Once he was out in the breakers, Nā-kaikua'ana seized the guns, knives, and gunpowder, including four large calabashes of pistols that had been left on the beach in his care. These were sent to Ka-umu-ali'i immediately.

Ki'i-kīkī saw his guns disappearing, but by the time he reached shore, it was too late. He hurried to Hanapēpē. He and his brother Kāne-'eku decided to leave Kaua'i. They fled to 'Ewa on O'ahu. Nā-kaikua'ana followed them and put them to death. Kaua'i was now securely in Ka-umu-ali'i's control.

Nā-kaikua'ana returned to Kaua'i with disturbing news. Kame-hameha, now ruler of all the windward islands, was preparing the largest war fleet ever assembled for a second attempt to conquer Kaua'i. He boasted to his followers, "Let us go and drink the water of Wailua, bathe in the water of Nā-molokama, eat the mullet that swim in Ka-wai-makua at Hā'ena, wreathe ourselves with the sea-lettuce of Polihale, then return to O'ahu and live there."

Just before the final preparations were finished, a malignant, quick-acting disease, thought to be either smallpox or bubonic plague, swept through Kamehameha's forces. So many died that there were no longer enough warriors for an invasion. Even Kameha-meha himself barely survived the disease. Kamehameha, however, never gave up the idea of adding Kaua'i to his kingdom.

Ka-umu-ali'i knew that only wily diplomacy would save his king-dom and his life. At age twenty-five, he stood alone against the might of Kamehameha. So when Kamehameha sent word to Ka-umu-ali'i that he would be satisfied if the Kaua'i chief would acknowledge Kamehameha as his sovereign and pay an annual tribute, Ka-umu-ali'i indicated that he would be willing to do this.

Kamehameha insisted that Ka-umu-ali'i come to O'ahu to make a public oath to accept Kamehameha as his overlord. Ka-umu-ali'i remembered the fate of Keōua, the Hawai'i chief who had been invited by Kamehameha to make peace but had been killed as he stepped ashore from his canoe and offered as a sacrifice in the new *heiau* built at Kawaihae. Ka-umu-ali'i assumed that Kamehameha intended the same fate for him and refused to go to O'ahu.

Kamehameha sent Kihei, one of his lesser chiefs, with a new invitation to come to O'ahu. Kihei was greeted by Ka-umu-ali'i with much pomp and circumstance. He was given wives and the *ahupua'a* of Kalihiwai. Kihei never returned to Kamehameha. He lived out his years in Kalihiwai and was buried within the walls of the *heaiu* he built there.

Ka-umu-ali'i sent a messenger of his own back, the chiefess Wahine-nui, with the message that he agreed with the treaty of peace but was unable to go to O'ahu at the time. He sent along many presents. Kamehameha, not to be outdone, gave Wahine-nui valuable presents to take back, including some large *peleleu* canoes and feather capes. With these went a message: "Tell Ka-umu-ali'i to visit me here on O'ahu." This was no longer an invitation, but an order.

Ka-umu-ali'i was caught on the horns of a dilemma. On one hand, all the visiting Western captains told him he could not oppose Kamehameha's forces and arms. Peace, they insisted, under Kamehameha's terms was the very best he could do. On the other hand, he was afraid he would meet Keōua's fate, and many of his chiefs were eager to test their prowess against an invader.

Hoping to stall negotiations as long as possible, Ka-umu-ali'i sent Pahiko, a close personal friend, with eleven double canoes and nine single canoes filled with presents for Kamehameha. A reminder of his own troubles in the Ka'ie'iewaho channel was sent to Kamehameha inadvertently, for all the canoes were swamped in a storm and only two made it to shore, one to O'ahu, the other to Ni'ihau.

Messengers continued to go to and fro. Many of Kamehameha's envoys were overwhelmed by the hospitality of Kaua'i and never left. Kaua'i envoys always returned home.

Finally Kamehameha sent Keawe-opu, Nāhili, and Isaac Davis.

Davis was a *haole* sailor whom Kamehameha had made a chief. Ka-umu-aliʻi had three trusted sailors in his own entourage who were loyal and whose advice had proved valuable. They listened to Davis. He made it clear that Ka-umu-aliʻi had no way out. He would have to go to Oʻahu.

Ka-umu-aliʻi sent his nephew Ka-mahole-lani, his wife, Nā-mahana, and two high chiefs, Hāʻupu and Kumumu, to make final arrangements for Ka-umu-aliʻi's coming. Ka-mahole-lani returned to Kauaʻi on board a vessel captained by Nathan Winship who had volunteered to provide transportation for the Kauaʻi ruler. Winship urged Ka-umu-aliʻi to meet with Kamehameha soon, before he became impatient and gave in to his chiefs who were agitating for an invasion. Captain Winship even offered to leave his first mate as a hostage on Kauaʻi as a promise of Ka-umu-aliʻi's safe return.

Ka-umu-aliʻi put his affairs in order. Five years earlier he had sent his oldest son George Humehume to New England to be educated in American ways but since then there had been no word from him. In any case, since his mother was of lower rank, Humehume could not become the paramount ruler. Ka-umu-aliʻi left the care of Kauaʻi in the hands of his sister-wife, Ka-puaʻa-mohu. He took only his favorite but childless wife, Ke-kai-haʻa-kūlou, with him.

Ka-umu-aliʻi first saw Oʻahu from the deck of Winship's ship. As the ship anchored off Honolulu, thirty-year-old Ka-umu-aliʻi dressed himself in his feathered helmet and cloak. He held a black piglet in his arms and waited with dignity for the coming of Kamehameha and, for all he knew, his death.

As soon as news reached Kamehameha that Ka-umu-aliʻi was coming, his *kahuna* Ka-ʻumi-ʻumi suggested: "The *lei palaoa* (ivory tusk necklace) has come here. Let the chief take the tusk." He meant, of course, to deal with Ka-umu-aliʻi as they had Keōua.

Kalai-kua-hulu, a *kahuna* noted for his skill in reciting genealogies, replied: "It would be a serious thing to have Kamehameha called the bloody-handed king because of the death of one who has been kind. I say the best thing for the king to do is to meet his kinsman, and when he comes to this island lay in his hand a fishhook and line, a symbol of the fish of the dark sea [Ka-umu-aliʻi] whom the king has brought hence. I say that Ka-umu-aliʻi shall not die in his own native haunt, but where he seizes the hook and line, there eventually shall his corpse be found."

Kamehameha agreed. "This is not the time of war," he said,

"which would justify me in killing another chief and seizing his possessions."

The landing place at Kakaka was crowded with the men and women who were to paddle Kamehameha and his chiefs out to the ship, as well as countless spectators. Kamehameha gave the signal and the huge double canoes sailed slowly out with pennants flying and drums beating. Kamehameha himself climbed into a four-man canoe. This single canoe paddled rapidly away from the other canoes and went beyond the ship until it reached the surf of Ka-kulu-aea. Then, when the other canoes had almost reached the American ship, Kamehameha's craft caught a wave and rode it triumphantly to come alongside the ship on the side away from the fleet.

It must have tickled Kamehameha's vanity to trick the Kaua'i chief in such a manner. When Kamehameha climbed aboard, however, Ka-umu-ali'i stood facing him. He had not been caught by surprise.

Ka-umu-ali'i spoke. "Here I am. Is it face up or face down?" Face up meant he would live, face down he would die.

Kamehameha replied, "Give me your hand."

"This is the gift at our meeting," Ka-umu-ali'i went on. "The land of Kaua'i, its chiefs, its men great and small, from mountain to sea, all above and below, and myself to be yours."

Kamehameha answered, "I shall not accept your land, not the least portion of your domain. Return and rule over it. But if your young chief makes you a visit, be pleased to receive him." By young chief, Kamehameha meant his son and heir, Liholiho.

Ka-umu-ali'i agreed and then said, "We have met and I am now returning."

Kamehameha insisted he stay. "Let us land. We have food and fish and wealth. Better come ashore." This was an order from a leader to his subordinate, and Ka-umu-ali'i gave in. On shore he and his wife Ke-kai-ha'a-kūlou were royally entertained and lavish gifts were given to them.

A few days later, Nā-'ihe, a member of Kamehameha's court, putting his plot to assassinate the Kaua'i ruler into motion, invited Ka-umu-ali'i to a feast to be held at Wai-ka-halulu, saying they would be serving rum, the latest intoxicant to come to Hawai'i. Ka-umu-ali'i had not yet tasted it.

Shortly before this feast was to be held, Ka-umu-ali'i paid a visit to Isaac Davis, whose blunt advice to submit to Kamehameha had swayed Ka-umu-ali'i. One reason for this visit was that Ka-umu-ali'i had been learning English and wanted to practice. As the two men were parting after a pleasant interlude, Davis said, "Do not go up to Wai-ka-halulu lest Nā-'ihe destroy you."

Startled, Ka-umu-ali'i prepared to go home. He had a last interview with Kamehameha and his prime minister, Ka-lani-moku. As they parted, Ka-lani-moku warned, "Take care of the chief Liholiho who belongs to you and to your cousin Ka-'ahu-manu. Liholiho shall be the heir."

Ka-umu-ali'i could only agree. He had come to O'ahu as a ruler; he was going home a vassal. Yet he had saved his kingdom from a bloodbath. It was the best he could do.

Soon after his return, Ka-umu-ali'i received word that Isaac Davis was dead. The conspirators under Nā-'ihe had poisoned him for warning Ka-umu-ali'i.

More and more ships kept coming, especially Yankee whalers and merchantmen. While the whalers hunted whales in Alaskan waters, the merchantmen sailed to China with holds full of sandalwood they had purchased from the Hawaiians. With this source of income, Kamehameha and Ka-umu-ali'i bought guns and ammunition. Ka-umu-ali'i hoped that someday, somehow, he could throw off Kamehameha's yoke. He did not have the resources that Kamehameha did, and the Hawai'i chief was able to gather more, including big swivel guns mounted on locally built ships. He had many muskets and rifles and a seemingly unlimited source of ammunition and gunpowder.

When the Russian ship *Bering* under Captain James Bennett stopped at Waimea in October 1814, Ka-umu-ali'i bought fifty muskets and forty-two rifles from him. Kaua'i was a long way from Kamehameha's court in Kailua, Hawai'i. Ka-umu-ali'i must have reasoned that if he could gather enough weaponry, Kaua'i might well free itself once more.

Guns were indeed welcome, but above all Ka-umu-ali'i needed Western ships. When the *Bering* returned to Waimea on January 31, 1815, and a storm drove the ship on shore, Ka-umu-ali'i promised to help Captain Bennett save his cargo but claimed the ship itself.

Captain Bennett could only agree. The *Bering* was full of seal skins, and these were taken ashore and stored in specially built huts at Makaweli. About two thousand men were gathered to try to save the *Bering*. The seas were too rough, and the ship broke to pieces. Some days later, Captain Bennett took passage in a passing ship and returned to Alaska to report to Alexander Baranov, chief manager of the Russian American Company.

Baranov made immediate plans to regain the cargo of seal skins. In October 1815 he hired the American ship *Isabella* and sent it to Hawai'i with a German doctor named Georg Scheffer on board as his agent. Scheffer was instructed to investigate the feasibility of establishing a Russian colony on the islands. Baranov understood the geographical value of these islands and realized that a colony where food for provisioning Russian ships could be grown would be useful to Russian interests in the Pacific Northwest.

Scheffer, however, took this one step further. He had dreams of leading a flourishing colony himself. He first landed at Kailua, presenting himself at Kamehameha's court. John Young, Kamehameha's trusted advisor, became suspicious of Scheffer's intentions. Scheffer moved on to Kaua'i.

His timing was excellent. When Scheffer landed at Waimea, Ka-umu-ali'i was ill with dropsy and one of his wives was down with a fever. Scheffer cured both quickly and earned the gratitude of the Kaua'i chief.

Scheffer hired two sailors living in Ka-umu-ali'i's court as his interpreters. He thought that they would keep his secrets in exchange for the presents he gave them. Rowbottom and Williams, however, had been with Ka-umu-ali'i for more than twenty years and were deeply loyal to him. They kept their chief fully informed of all they learned.

At first everyone thought Scheffer was there simply to trade. Soon the doctor began to disclose his intentions to establish a colony, assist the Kaua'i chief to gain possession of all the islands, and prevent American ships from trading anywhere in the islands. He promised to sell Ka-umu-ali'i a ship or two.

Ka-umu-ali'i seized this opportunity. He thought Scheffer was an official envoy of the Russians and swore allegiance to the Tsar Alexander I. He returned the *Bering*'s cargo of seal skins and paid an indemnity for them, since Scheffer claimed the skins had been damaged. In addition, Scheffer got permission to build trading posts.

Scheffer was given land in Waimea. He immediately began to

build a fort overlooking the town. Scheffer began a vineyard, grew melons and tobacco, and discovered that wheat did not grow well. He thought cotton would become the chief produce of the island, and in both Hanalei and Waimea cotton fields flourished for a time.

Scheffer had two supply ships that Baranov had rented. Scheffer felt no compunction in selling one of them, the *Lydia*, to Ka-umu-ali'i who paid in sandalwood as well as giving Scheffer the *ahupua'a* of Hanalei. This the doctor promptly renamed Schefferthal and began to build two forts there that he manned with the Aleutian islanders he had brought with him.

Then Scheffer overreached himself. He sent some men and a ship to O'ahu and began to build a fort and trading post at Honolulu Harbor. Kamehameha, alarmed, ordered Ka-lani-moku, his chief advisor, to send the interloper packing. At this moment, the Russian brig *Rurik*, under Captain Otto von Kotzebue, arrived at Kailua. Captain von Kotzebue rescinded everything Scheffer was doing. It was all a private matter of the German doctor, von Kotzebue said, and nothing to do with official Russian activities.

Scheffer remained on Kaua'i for five more months. He thought he was secure. When Kamehameha sent orders to rid Kaua'i of this menace, Ka-umu-ali'i could only obey. Scheffer was forcibly escorted on board his ship, the *Kodiak*. There was a plot to drown the doctor and holes were drilled in the boat that took him from shore to his ship, but the doctor arrived on board—wet but alive.

Scheffer and his men attempted to come ashore the following day to regain their lost property, but they were fired upon from the guns in the fort they themselves had built. Scheffer sailed away to Hanalei.

News reached Hanalei before Scheffer. The Hanalei warriors attacked the fort, killed two of the Aleuts, took the rest captive, and drove off Scheffer's cattle. Now warriors were gathered on the beach to prevent the Russians from landing. Taking the Aleuts on board, Scheffer sailed on to Honolulu where he took the first ship out. He never returned to Hawai'i or to Alaska for that matter.

The Russian flag flew over Kaua'i for a brief time, as the English, French, and American flags had flown from time to time over the court of Kamehameha. Ka-umu-ali'i tried to free Kaua'i and was lucky that Kamehameha did not send anyone to closely question his actions, which could easily be seen as treason.

Ka-umu-ali'i continued as the vassal ruler. In 1817 Kamehameha bought the ship *Columbia* to add to his fleet. The owners were paid in sandalwood, twice the amount its hold could carry. The chief of the Waimea and Wai'anae districts of O'ahu and Ka-umu-ali'i of Kaua'i were ordered to provide the sandalwood.

In the next two years Ka-umu-ali'i bought cloth, muskets, powder, and several ships, two large ones called *Kamohelani* and *Mika-pako,* as well as several smaller ones. Every purchase was paid in sandalwood.

In 1819 Kamehameha died. Only his forceful, powerful, charismatic widow Ka-'ahu-manu held the kingdom together. Within a few months, she ended the ancient *kapu* system, the foundation on which the power of the *ali'i* rested. There was a new power base, that of hereditary rulers, the heirs of Kamehameha.

In 1820, missionaries bearing the Calvin-based Congregational beliefs arrived in the islands. They brought with them Ka-umu-ali'i's son Humehume, long given up for lost.

George Humehume was the oldest son of Ka-umu-ali'i, born to a woman of lesser rank. He could never inherit the kingdom; that honor belonged to Ke-ali'i-aho-nui, son of Ka-umu-ali'i and his half-sister Ka-pua'a-mohu.

In 1805, Ka-umu-ali'i had placed Humehume, who was seven or eight at the time, in the care of a Yankee captain, with enough goods to maintain the boy through years of schooling and eventual return home. Soon after arriving in New England, the captain died, his creditors seized all the money, and Humehume was turned out into the streets. He wandered for several years. When the War of 1812 began, he enlisted in the Navy and was wounded in battle. When the doctors discovered he was underage, he was discharged and dumped ashore. He was found without resources in the naval yards of Charleston, Massachusetts. He was sent to the Congregational school in Cornwall, Connecticut, where several other Hawaiian boys were.

He studied there for many years, but he enjoyed his escapades and his drinking and never took to the religious teachings. He was popular, for he had a fine voice and played the bass viol. He insisted on being called Prince George.

When the first Congregational missionaries left for Hawai'i, they took Humehume with them. Two of the missionaries, Samuel Whitney and Samuel Ruggles, accompanied Humehume to Kaua'i.

Ka-umu-ali'i greeted his son and the two missionaries with open arms. The missionaries were given land and help in building a church and school. Ka-umu-ali'i himself learned to read and write in English and converted to Congregationalism.

Humehume was installed as the chief of the Waimea *ahupua'a,* but he became addicted to alcohol. In a short time, he was banished to Wahiawa and lived in poverty.

There was always the danger that Liholiho and Ka-'ahu-manu would demand that Ka-umu-ali'i cede Kaua'i entirely to them. There was a constant danger to his life, for only Ka-umu-ali'i stood between the rapacious Kamehamehas and Kaua'i's freedom. He wanted to live in peace. In early summer 1821, Ka-umu-ali'i prepared his brig *Becket,* which he had just bought. He intended to sail to Tahiti as his ancestors Kiha and La'a-mai-Kahiki had done and find a home there.

He suggested to Rev. Hiram Bingham that two missionaries should make the journey with him. Bingham went to Honolulu and consulted with his co-workers. They agreed that one of their number from Kaua'i should accept the king's generous offer. The missionaries wanted to obtain copies of all publications printed in the Tahitian language, which would help them in Hawai'i. They also wanted to see firsthand what results the southern missionaries had had evangelizing a people that possessed a great similarity of character, habits, language, customs, conditions, and religion.

Bingham went to get the approval of Liholiho and Ka-'ahu-manu. Ka-'ahu-manu's curiosity was aroused. She decided to send a personal message to Pomare, the king of Tahiti, and to send a present of sheets of *kapa* and a feather cloak. In return, she asked that she be given sea shells, polished coconut shells, a surfboard, and seeds of any food plants that were not found in Hawai'i.

Then she went to Kaua'i for the first time. Ka-umu-ali'i and and his wife Ke-kai-ha'a-kūlou (now known as Deborah Kapule since her conversion to Christianity) met her on the beach at Luhi, in front of the mission house, which then stood directly between the sea and the fort. They embraced, lifted up their voices in chants and wept. Then they feasted on hogs, dogs, and fowl.

While the Kaua'i court and its visitors surfed in the waves, another visitor came from Honolulu. John C. Jones, the United States commercial agent, strongly objected to the proposed trip to Tahiti. He said that the American missionaries should not be getting help from the English, nor was it good for the mission to be so obligated to Ka-umu-ali'i, and since the Tahitian and Hawaiian languages were so different, books from there would be no help in Hawai'i. Jones played this kind of role when the Russians were attempting to found a colony on O'ahu, and he felt sure his arguments would also prevail this time.

Meanwhile Liholiho decided to visit Kaua'i, but told no one else of his plans. He said he was going for a visit to 'Ewa from Waikīkī and set out in an undecked sailboat. His wife, Kapi'olani, and his friends Nā-'ihe and Boki joined him for the brief excursion down the coast. Liholiho refused to land and the little overcrowded boat, without water, food, compass or any other navigational aid, sailed into the rough and dangerous channel between the islands.

His passengers begged him to return to O'ahu. Night fell, and they were nearly capsized as a large wave washed over them, filling the boat with water.

"Turn around," his passengers pleaded.

Liholiho replied, "No. Bail out the water and go on." Just before dawn they reached the Waimea roads. Ka-umu-ali'i was waiting on the beach with three unarmed men.

Ka-umu-ali'i sent word to Honolulu that Liholiho was safe. Boki's wife, Liliha, sailed to Kaua'i in a single canoe propelled by a small white sail and four rowers with broad paddles.

On July 24, 1821, Ka-umu-ali'i formally offered to give Liholiho the island of Kaua'i, all his vessels, the fort and the guns. For a time Liholiho did not answer, and the silence must have caused dread in the Kaua'i hearts.

Finally Liholiho replied. "I did not come to dispossess you," he told Ka-umu-ali'i. "Keep your land and take care of it as before, and do what you please with your vessels." The Kauaians cheered and made plans to let Liholiho see for himself the beauties of Kaua'i and indulge in the famous Kaua'i hospitality.

As a token of these newly established friendly relations, Ke-kai-ha'a-kūlou, Ka-umu-ali'i's favorite wife, was given to Liholiho. She was young, beautiful, and childless. The queen dowager Ka-'ahumanu was not pleased when she heard this and came to Kaua'i.

When Liholiho's five other wives arrived from O'ahu on board the *Ha'aheo o Hawai'i*, Liholiho, his court, and all the principal chiefs of Kaua'i traveled around the island. This trip lasted forty-two days.

During the entertainment one evening, the name of Nihoa island was sung. No one had ever seen this island, and on a whim Ka-umu-ali‘i and Ka-‘ahu-manu boarded his ship the *Becket* and sailed to Nihoa. On their return to Waimea, Bingham demanded to know when Ka-umu-ali‘i was sailing for Tahiti. Ka-umu-ali‘i promised that they would sail in six days.

The following Sabbath, the two kings went on board their respective brigs and had a sailing race. Anchoring at evening, Ka-umu-ali‘i joined Liholiho for dinner. During the meal, Liholiho signalled his captain. The anchor and sails of *Ha‘aheo o Hawai‘i* were quietly raised, and the ship sailed for O‘ahu. Ka-umu-ali‘i was a prisoner.

The following morning, Hā‘upu, *konohiki* chief of Waimea *ahu-pua‘a* and father of Ke-kai-ha‘a-kūlou, wept. "Farewell to our chief," he said. "We shall see him no more."

To cement the Kamehameha power, Ka-umu-ali‘i was compelled to marry the dowager queen, Ka-‘ahu-manu on October 9, 1821. She also married Ka-umu-ali‘i's son and heir, Ke-ali‘i-aho-nui. From then on, wherever Ka-‘ahu-manu went, the Kaua‘i chiefs were kept at her side.

Many of Ka-umu-ali‘i's *ali‘i* joined him in exile on O‘ahu. Ka-lani-moku, Ka-‘ahu-manu's right-hand man, announced that Ka-umu-ali‘i's sister, Wahine-nui, would be governor of Kaua‘i in the absence of the king. The real ruler was Ka-lani-moku.

On May 26, 1824, Ka-umu-ali‘i lay dying in Ka-‘ahu-manu's house in Honolulu. His family had been allowed to come from Kaua‘i—his sisters were there, his daughter Kapo and his son George Humehume. Even his former wife Ke-kai-ha‘a-kūlou had come to be with him. None of them, however, were permitted to see him before he died.

Ka-‘ahu-manu and Ka-lani-moku hovered over the deathbed, demanding that Ka-umu-ali‘i name an heir.

Ka-lani-moku demanded, "After your death, who is to be your successor?"

Ka-umu-ali‘i replied, "Our son." By this, they understood he meant Liholiho.

Then came an important question as far as the Kamehamehas were concerned. "How about the lands?"

"Let the lands be as they are; those chiefs who have lands to hold them, those who have not to have none." With those words, Ka-umu-ali'i condemned his people in a way he could not have fore-seen.

He was given a magnificent funeral, and his body was taken in state to Maui where he is buried next to Ke-ōpū-o-lani, one of the wives of Kamehameha.

'Ai-pua'a, the Rebellion of 1824

When Deborah Kapule (no longer called Ke-kai-ha'a-kūlou) returned to Waimea, she was met by a huge crowd, demanding the details of their king's death and funeral. Already many people had knocked out a front tooth in sorrowful memory of their late king.

George Humehume also returned to Kaua'i, suffering from an unknown ailment. He was convinced that he had been poisoned by Ka-'ahu-manu.

Meanwhile it was generally expected that Ka-umu-ali'i's son Ke-ali'i-aho-nui would be named governor of Kaua'i, replacing his father in that position. Given this opportunity, however, the Kamehamehas did not hesitate. Ka-hala-i'a, a nephew of Ka-lani-moku, was appointed instead.

Ka-hala-i'a was, says Rev. Hiram Bingham, "young, well formed, above the middling stature, fond of amusements and worldly plea-sure, bold and ambitious, and more distinguished for energy than honor, sobriety, or love of equity and peace."

The day after he arrived he inspected Fort Hipo, built by the Rus-sians overlooking the Waimea river mouth. He found fifty guns and enough muskets, bayonets, and swords to arm a guard. In no time at all, he demonstrated that he considered Kaua'i a conquered territory and he a victorious spoiler.

On June 26, 1824, before the official mourning period had ended, there was a total eclipse of the sun at one o'clock in the afternoon. To quote Bingham again: "The gloom of the moon's shadow on the islands corresponded with the political gloom that then hung over Kaua'i, while many of the inhabitants lived in apprehension of evils, against which they had no competent protection. Some feared oppression from the windward chiefs, should their control be undis-puted. Others feared oppression of destruction from Kaua'i chiefs, now divided into parties. Some, decidedly favoring the new order, provoked the envy and hostility of those who disliked to yield to windward supremacy. The want of integrity, and of the means of intelligence and intercommunication, magnified the difficulty; and distrust, disaffection, and danger, seemed to envelope the island in clouds."

Kaua'i chief Kia'i-makani demanded that the lands on the island be thrown together as had always been done in the past and a new division made. Ka-lani-moku refused, saying only, "Let us abide by the charge of the late king."

Kia'i-makani spoke of the strife within the kingdom of Kaua'i before Ka-umu-ali'i became king. He told of Keawe kidnapping his younger half-brother, and how Ki'ikīkī had shot Keawe and how Ka-umu-ali'i had ordered the death of Ki'ikīkī. Each time the lands had been divided anew. Ka-lani-moku refused to budge. One of the Kamehameha men insulted Kia'i-makani, and he angrily left.

A call went out from Waimea for all of the chiefs of Kaua'i to gather with their tribute and offerings to the Kamehameha family, personified by Ka-lani-moku. George Humehume left his home but was intercepted by Kia'i-makani who had gathered some warriors. "You shall not pay homage," Kia'i-makani told George, "neither will we. Come with us and you shall be our king. The island is yours as it was your father's. You shall be king, and we are your nā koa, the warriors. Many will fight for you."

George Humehume could not resist the temptation. On the morning of August 8, he led the attack on Fort Hipo. The battle lasted thirty minutes.

The insurgents, with only their ancient weapons, were no match for modern arms and ammunition. They fled toward Hanapēpē. Several insurgents were captured and one, Ka-maka-kini, was tied hand and foot and hauled onto Ka-lani-moku's ship. The missionary families were hurried on board, too, and the message of war on Kaua'i was sent to Honolulu. During the night, Ka-maka-kini was thrown overboard.

Ka-lani-moku prepared his troops and marched on Hanapēpē. On the Wahiawa plains the insurgents faced him with their wooden spears and daggers. The Kamehameha large guns fired across the battlefield and the insurgents' line broke. Kia'i-makani was killed, and his body was treated with great indignity. George Humehume fled for the mountains with his wife and child.

For two weeks Ka-lani-moku searched the island, and every ali'i man, woman, and child in any way connected with the rebellion was slaughtered. Their bodies were left as food for the pigs, and this

Rebellion of 1824 was called 'Ai-pua'a (*Pig eater*) by the victorious Kamehameha forces.

Humehume was found three weeks later. He was taken to Honolulu. In two years he was dead from an imported disease.

When Hoapili, Kamehameha's close friend, and Ka-iki-o-'Ewa, his cousin, arrived at the head of fresh forces, they found the island subdued and cowed. Ka-lani-moku at last declared an end to the rebellion. By that time the Kaua'i *ali'i* were either dead, in permanent exile on Maui, or had disappeared into the ranks of the *maka-'āinana*, the commoners, in order to survive.

On August 27, Ka-'ahu-manu herself arrived. Liholiho was in England, and she was the de facto supreme ruler of all the islands. The words of Samuel Kamakau say it best: "The lands were again divided. Soldiers who had been given lands but had returned to O'ahu had their lands taken away, chiefs who had large lands were deprived of them, and the *palaualelo* (loafers and hangers-on) of O'ahu and Maui obtained the rich lands of Kaua'i."

One of the Kaua'i warriors on the Wahiawa plains that fateful day was Nā-koa-ola. His wife, Pāmahoā, stood beside him. They fought as best they could, but all too soon Nā-koa-ola died of a rifle shot. Pāmahoā, that evening, removed his body from the battlefield and stripped the flesh from his bones. She wove a covered basket in which to store his bones, and this bundle she always carried with her as she wandered, half-crazed, from one side of the island to another.

She wandered into the room where Ka-'ahu-manu was visiting with Deborah Kapule at Wailua. Ka-'ahu-manu had come to Kaua'i only to divide the rich lands among her own family and a few of her toadies. But in coming into the imperious presence, Pāmahoā broke a *kapu*. Enraged, Ka-'ahu-manu ordered the guards to take the woman out and kill her.

The two guards, however, were Kaua'i men. They seized Pāmahoā and pushed her up the Kuamo'o trail away from the dreaded Ka-'ahu-manu. At the top, they let go of her. One guard said, "Run. Do not come back." Pāmahoā, her bundle clasped fiercely to her, ran. She reached the crossing above the great Wailua waterfall. As she stepped from one slippery stone to the next, she glanced down into the pool below and saw her husband's reflection beckoning to her. With a cry that still echoes there, Pāmahoā leaped.

With that cry, the independent kingdom of Kaua'i came to an end.

GENEALOGIES

THE KUMU-HONUA GENEALOGY

[cf. Fornander, *Polynesian Race*, pp. 181–183]

The history of Kauaʻi's *aliʻi nui* begins with the creation of the first man, Kumu-honua, and the first woman, Lalo-honua, who were created by the four paramount gods of Polynesia, Kāne, Kanaloa, Lono, and Kū. There had been countless generations before Kumu-honua, but as all Polynesian history had to be remembered and narrated by specially trained men and women, the burden of names and adventures became too much and a new beginning had to be made.

The Kumu-honua Genealogy is the lineage of the Earth Mother, Papa-nui-hānau-moku. It covers about 925 years of history. In thirty-six generations, tales are told of only five: Laka, Kini-lau-a-mano, Ke-ao-melemele, Nuʻu, and Hawaiʻi-loa. Papa-nui-hānau-moku is considered to be the progenitor of the Polynesian people.

For the convenience of the modern reader, it is arbitrarily assumed here that there are four generations each century. Dating begins with the birth of Ka-umu-aliʻi, which is known to have occurred in 1780, and each generation is counted backwards in twenty-five–year increments. The dates are by no means correct, for people do not live and die in twenty-five–year intervals. In addition there are variants in the genealogies, sometimes major differences. Since the Polynesians kept track of time only through the genealogies of their chiefs, such variants didn't matter.

	PARENTS		OFFSPRING
1. (370 B.C.)	Kumuhonua, *k*	Lalohonua, *w*	Laka, *k*
2. (345 B.C.)	Laka, *k*	Papaialaka, *w*	Kamoolewa, *k*
3. (320 B.C.)	Kamoolewa, *k*	Olepuuhonua, *w*	Maluapo, *k*
4. (295 B.C.)	Maluapo, *k*	Laweao, *w*	Kinilauamano, *k*
5. (270 B.C.)	Kinilauamano, *k*	Upolu, *w*	Halo, *k*
6. (245 B.C.)	Halo, *k*	Kiniewalu, *w*	Kamanolani, *k*
7. (220 B.C.)	Kamanolani, *k*	Kalanianoho, *w*	Kamakaokalani, *k*
8. (195 B.C.)	Kamakaokalani, *k*	Kamoolani, *w*	Kaleilani, *k*
9. (170 B.C.)	Kaleilani, *k*	Opuahiki, *w*	Kalalii, *k*
10. (145 B.C.)	Kalalii, *k*	Kaaomelemele, *w*	Haule, *k*
11. (120 B.C.)	Haule, *k*	Loaaio, *w*	Iminanea, *k*
12. (95 B.C.)	Iminanea, *k*	Imiwalea, *w*	Nuu, *k*
13. (70 B.C.)	Nuu, *k*	Lilinoe, *w*	Naluakua, *k*
14. (45 B.C.)	Naluakua, *k*	Kaaliakea, *w*	Naeheehelani, *k*
15. (20 B.C.)	Naeheehelani, *k*	Kawowoilanihikimoe, *w*	Kahakuimokulei, *k*
16. (5 A.D.)	Kahakuimokulei, *k*	Kekaiholana, *w*	Kekailei, *k*
17. (30 A.D.)	Kekailei, *k*	Nalulei, *w*	Kahakulani, *k*
18. (55 A.D.)	Kahakulani, *k*	Moeanailalo, *w*	Heleikahikiku, *k*
19. (80 A.D.)	Heleikahikiku, *k*	Hooneeneeikahikina, *w*	Kanoelohikina, *k*
20. (105 A.D.)	Kanoelohikina, *k*	Halapoloa, *w*	Heleikamooloa, *k*

[*k* indicates *kāne* (male) and *w* indicates *wahine* (female).]

	PARENTS		OFFSPRING
21. (130 A.D.)	Heleikamooloa, *k*	Kaweheaao, *w*	Keauapaapaa, *k*
22. (155 A.D.)	Keauapaapaa, *k*	Keaulaelae, *w*	Luanuu, *k*
23. (180 A.D.)	Luanuu, *k*	Meehiwa, *w*	Kalanimenehune, *k*
24. (205 A.D.)	Kalanimenehune, *k*	Kamolehikinakuahine, *w*	Iaimipukaku, *k*
25. (230 A.D.)	Iaimipukaku, *k*	Kahooluhikupaa, *w*	Newenewemaolinai-kahikiku, *k*
26. (255 A.D.)	Newenewemaolinai-kahikiku, *k*	Nowelohikina, *w*	Kaokaokalani, *k*
27. (280 A.D.)	Kaokaokalani, *k*	Hehakamoku, *w*	Anianiku, *k*
28. (305 A.D.)	Anianiku, *k*	Kekaipahola, *w*	Anianikalani, *k*
29. (330 A.D.)	Anianikalani, *k*	Kameenuihikina, *w*	Hawaiiloa, *k*
30. (355 A.D.)	Hawaiiloa, *k*	Hualalai, *w*	Oahu, *w*
31. (380 A.D.)	Oahu, w	Kunuiaiakeakua, *k*	Kunuiakea, *k*
32. (405 A.D.)	Kunuiakea, *k*	Kahikiwalea, *w*	Keliialia, *k*
33. (430 A.D.)	Keliialia, *k*	Kahikialii, *w*	Kemilia, *k*
34. (455 A.D.)	Kemilia, *k*	Polohainalii, *w*	Keliiku, *k*
35. (480 A.D.)	Keliiku, *k*	Kaoupealii, *w*	Kukalaniehu, *k*
36. (505 A.D.)	Kukalaniehu, *k*	Kahakauakoko, *w*	Papanuihanaumoku, *w*
37. (530 A.D.)	Papanuihanaumoku, *w*	Wakea, *k*	

Papa-nui-hānau-moku is thought to have lived either in Fiji, Samoa, or Tonga. From one of these island groups, she led her people into the Pacific Ocean where they discovered the famed islands of the South Pacific: Nukuhiwa, Ra'iātea, Tahiti, and, in time, the islands of the Hawaiian archipelago.

THE BROKEN GENEALOGY

The first known settlers of Kaua'i claimed descent from Papa-nui-hānau-moku through her son Ka-māwae-lua-lani-moku. The Kū'alu family sent back to their homeland for the Menehune, a people who claimed direct descent from Ka-lani-menehune (Kumu-honua, generation 24). The Lohi family brought the Mū or Nawao people who descended from Kū-nawao, brother of Ka-lani-menehune. The descendants of Kū'alu-nui-kini-akua eventually were absorbed by vigorous newcomers from the south. Thus their genealogy was forgotten and can only be pieced together through the few legends that survive from this early time.

	PARENTS		OFFSPRING
(530 A.D.)	Papanuihanaumoku, *w*	Wakea, *k*	Kamawaelualanimoku, *k*
(555 A.D.)	Kamawaelualanimoku, *k*		

The Kūʻalu Family

	Kualunuikiniakua, *k*	[unknown]	Kualunuipaukumokumoku, *k*
	Kualunuipaukumokumoku, *k*	Kahapula, *w*	Ola, *k*
	Ola, *k*		

The Lohi Family

	Lohi, *k*	Lohipono, *w*	Kanealohi, *k*
	Kanealohi, *k*	[unknown]	Kalaulehua, *k*
	Kalaulehua, *k*		

The Last Chiefs of the Kona Kingdom

(1205 A.D.)	Kaikipaananea, *k*		
- - - - - - -			
(1330 A.D.)	Kekoaola, *k*		
- - - - - - -			
(1405 A.D.)	Makaliinuikuakawaiea, *k*	[unknown]	Naekapulani, *w*

[*k* indicates *kane* (male) and *w* indicates *wahine* (female).]

Makaliʻi-nui-kū-a-ka-wai-ea's daughter Nae-kapu-lani married Mano-ka-lani-pō, the son of Kūkona who had defeated her father and won his kingdom.

THE NANA-'ULU GENEALOGY FROM
PAPA-NUI-HĀNAU-MOKU TO KI'I

According to David Malo, the first six generations after Papa-nui-hānau-moku lived in O-lolo-i-mehani, an island that can no longer be identified. In the twelve generations between Papa-nui-hānau-moku, Nukuhiwa (the Marquesas Islands) was settled by voyagers either from Samoa or Fiji. In turn, Nukuhiwa sent out voyagers who found the Society Islands to the south. Ki'i was a chief of Tahiti. His son 'Ulu is credited with the discovery and settlement of islands to the west of Tahiti as he searched for the way back to Papa-nui-hānau-moku's homeland. Ki'i's other son Nana-'ulu sailed north and found the Hawaiian Islands, which were already settled by people claiming descent from Ka-lani-menehune (number 24, Kumu-honua Genealogy). They had already settled Nihoa, Neckar, Ni'ihau, and Kaua'i.

	PARENTS		OFFSPRING
1. (530 A.D.)	Papanuihanaumoku, *w*	Wakea, *k*	Hoohokukalani, *w*
2. (555 A.D.)	Hoohokukalani, *w*	Manouluae, *k*	Waia, *k*
3. (580 A.D.)	Waia, *k*	Huhune, *w*	Wailoa, *k*
4. (605 A.D.)	Wailoa, *k*	Hikawaopualanea, *w*	Kakaihili, *k*
5. (630 A.D.)	Kakaihili, *k*	Haulani, *w*	Kia, *k*
6. (655 A.D.)	Kia, *k*	Kamole, *w*	Ole, *k*
7. (680 A.D.)	Ole, *k*	Haii, *w*	Pupue, *k*
8. (705 A.D.)	Pupue, *k*	Kamahele, *w*	Manaku, *k*
9. (730 A.D.)	Manaku, *k*	Hikohaale, *w*	Nukahakoa, *k*
10. (755 A.D.)	Nukahakoa, *k*	Koulamaikalani, *w*	Luanuu, *k*
11. (780 A.D.)	Luanuu, *k*	Kawaamaukele, *w*	Kahiko, *k*
12. (805 A.D.)	Kahiko, *k*	Kaea, *w*	Kii, *k*
13. (830 A.D.)	Kii, *k*	Hinakoula, *w*	Ulu, *k*
			Nanaulu, *k*

[*k* indicates *kane* (male) and *w* indicates *wahine* (female).]

THE NANA-'ULU GENEALOGY FROM KI'I TO MO'IKEHA

[cf. Fornander, *Polynesian Race*, I:188]

All *ali'i*, the elite class, from Kaua'i and O'ahu from the time of Maweke (no. 29) could trace their ancestry back to Nana-'ulu. The *mana* or spiritual power descending through the Kaua'i chiefs was always considered stronger than any other because it was the most ancient genealogy known. Legends are silent concerning the first of these chiefs to arrive in the Hawaiian Islands, but Nana-'ulu's grandson Peheke-'ula (no. 16) is said to have been a ruling chief of O'ahu. Maweke (no. 29) came from Ra'iātea, and his grandsons and great-grandsons often sailed back and forth between Hawai'i and Ra'iātea.

	PARENTS		OFFSPRING
13. (830 A.D.)	Kii, k	Hinakoula, w	Nanaulu, k
14. (855 A.D.)	Nanaulu, k	Ulukou, w	Nanamea, k
15. (880 A.D.)	Nanamea, k	Puia, w	Pehekeula, k
16. (905 A.D.)	Pehekeula, k	Uluae, w	Pehekemana, k
17. (930 A.D.)	Pehekemana, k	Nanahapa, w	Nanamua, k
18. (955 A.D.)	Nanamua, k	Nanahope, w	Nanaikeauhaku, k
19. (980 A.D.)	Nanaikeauhaku, k	Elehu, w	Keaoa, k
20. (1005 A.D.)	Keaoa, k	Waohala, w	Hekumu, k
21. (1030 A.D.)	Hekumu, k	Kumukoa, w	Umalei, k
22. (1055 A.D.)	Umalei, k	Umaumanana, w	Kalai, k
23. (1080 A.D.)	Kalai, k	Laikapa, w	Malelewaa, k
24. (1105 A.D.)	Malelewaa, k	Pililohai, w	Hopoe, k
25. (1130 A.D.)	Hopoe, k	Kauananaia, w	Makalawena, k
26. (1155 A.D.)	Makalawena, k	Koihouhoua, w	Lelehooma, k
27. (1180 A.D.)	Lelehooma, k	Hapuu, w	Kekupahaikala, k
28. (1205 A.D.)	Kekupahaikala, k	Maihikea, w	Maweke, k
29. (1230 A.D.)	Maweke, k	Naiolaukea, w	Mulielealii, k
			Kalehenui, k
			Keaunui, k
30. (1255 A.D.)	Mulielealii, k	Wehelani, w	Kumuhonua, k
			Olopana, k
			Moikeha, k
			Hainakolo, w
31. (1280 A.D.)	Moikeha, k	Hinaaulua, w	Hookamalii, k
			Haulaninuiaiakea, k
			Kila, k

[k indicates *kane* (male) and w indicates *wahine* (female).]

THE 'ULU GENEALOGY FROM KI'I
TO LA'A-MAI-KAHIKI

[cf. Fornander, *Polynesian Race*, pp. 190–191]

Today there is no way to reconcile the 'Ulu and the Nana-'ulu genealogies, as the 'Ulu line contains at least seven more generations than the other. This line contains the famous trickster Māui-ki'iki'i as well as the Hema–Laka line, which gave rise to so many legends that the genealogists reciting Paumakua's ancestry may well have included them because of their renown. Paumakua was born in the south and migrated to Hawai'i at the same time as Maweke (no. 29 of the Nana-'ulu line).

	PARENTS		OFFSPRING
13. (830 A.D.)	Kii, *k*	Hinakoula, *w*	Ulu, *k*
14. (855 A.D.)	Ulu, *k*	Kapunuu, *w*	Nanaie, *k*
15. (880 A.D.)	Nanaie, *k*	Kahaumokuleia, *w*	Nanailani, *k*
16. (905 A.D.)	Nanailani, *k*	Hinakinau, *w*	Waikulani, *k*
17. (930 A.D.)	Waikulani, *k*	Kekauilani, *w*	Kuheleimoana, *k*
18. (955 A.D.)	Kuheleimoana, *k*	Mapunaiaala, *w*	Konohiki, *k*
19. (980 A.D.)	Konohiki, *k*	Hikaululena, *w*	Wawena, *k*
20. (1005 A.D.)	Wawena, *k*	Hinamahuia, *w*	Akalana, *k*
21.	Akalana, *k*	Hina-kawea, *w*	Mauiakalana, *k*
			Mauikiikii, *k*
22.	Mauiakalana, *k*	Hinakealohaila, *w*	Nanamaoa, *k*
23.	Nanamaoa, *k*	Hinaikapaikua, *w*	Nanakulei, *k*
24.	Nanakulei, *k*	Kahaukuhonua, *w*	Nanakaoko, *k*
25.	Nanakaoko, *k*	Kahihiokalani, *w*	Heleipawa, *k*
26.	Heleipawa, *k*	Kookookumaikalani, *w*	Hulumanailani, *k*
27.	Hulumanailani, *k*	Hinamaikalani, *w*	Aikanakaamakoo, *k*
28.	Aikanakaamakoo, *k*	Hinahanaiakamalama, *w*	Hema, *k*
			Puna, *k*
29.	Hema, *k*	Ulumahahoa, *w*	Kahai, *k*
30.	Kahai, *k*	Hinauluohia, *w*	Wahieloa, *k*
31.	Wahieloa, *k*	Koolaukahili, *w*	Laka, *k*
32.	Laka, *k*	Hikawaelena, *w*	Luanuu, *k*
33.	Luanuu, *k*	Kapokulaiula, *w*	Kamea, *k*
34.	Kamea, *k*	Popomaili, *w*	Pohukaina, *k*
35.	Pohukaina, *k*	Huahuakapalei, *w*	Hua, *k*
36.	Hua, *k*	Hikimolulolea, *w*	Pau, *k*
37.	Pau, *k*	Kapohaakia, *w*	Huanuikalalailai, *k*
38.	Huanuikalalailai, *k*	Kapoea, *w*	Paumakua, *k*
39. (1255 A.D.)	Paumakua, *k*	Manokalililani, *w*	

[*k* indicates *kane* (male) and *w* indicates *wahine* (female).]

No genealogy survives to show how Laʻa-mai-Kahiki is descended from Paumakua.

GENEALOGY FROM LA'A-MAI-KAHIKI
TO KAWELO-'AI-KANAKA

[cf. Fornander, *Polynesian Race*, I:248]

No genealogy has survived to show how La'a-mai-Kahiki descended from Paumakua (no. 39 of the 'Ulu line), but every legend states he was Paumakua's grandson and that he was *hānai* (adopted) by Mo'i-keha (no. 31 of the Nana-'ulu line). La'a-mai-Kahiki's son Ahukini-a-La'a is followed by fourteen generations in an unbroken line of ruling chiefs of Kaua'i.

	PARENTS		OFFSPRING
32. (1305 A.D.)	Laamaikahiki, k	Waolena, w	Ahukinialaa, k
33. (1330 A.D.)	Ahukinialaa, k	Haiakamaio, w	Kamahano, k
34. (1355 A.D.)	Kamahano, k	Kaaueanuiokalani, w	Luanuu, k
35. (1380 A.D.)	Luanuu, k	Kalanimoeikawaikai, w	Kukona, k
36. (1405 A.D.)	Kukona, k	Laupuapuamaa, w	Manokalanipo, k
37. (1430 A.D.)	Manokalanipo, k	Naekapulani, w	Kaumakaamano, k
38. (1455 A.D.)	Kaumakaamano, k	Kapoinukai, w	Kahakuakane, k
39. (1480 A.D.)	Kahakuakane, k	Manukaikoo, w	Kuwalupaukamoku, k
40. (1505 A.D.)	Kuwalupaukamoku, k	Hameawahaula, w	Kahakumakapaweo, k
41. (1530 A.D.)	Kahakumakapaweo, k	Kahakukukanea, w	Kalanikukuma, k
42. (1555 A.D.)	Kalanikukuma, k	Kapoleikauila, w	Kahakumakalina, k
43. (1580 A.D.)	Kahakumakalina, k	Kahakumaia, w	Kamakapu, k
44. (1605 A.D.)	Kamakapu, k	Pawahine, w	Kawelomahamahaia, k
45. (1630 A.D.)	Kawelomahamahaia, k	Kapohinakalani, w	Kawelomakalua, k
46. (1655 A.D.)	Kawelomakalua, k	Kaawihikalani, w, pi'o	Kawelopeekoa, k
			Kaweloaikanaka, k
47. (1680 A.D.)	Kaweloaikanaka, k	Naki, w	

[k indicates *kane* (male) and w indicates *wahine* (female).]

THE GENEALOGY FROM KA-KUHI-HEWA
TO KA-UMU-ALI'I

[cf. Fornander, *Polynesian Race*, II: 92–95, 291–298]

After both Kawelo-'ai-kanaka and his cousin Kawelo-lei-makua
died, there was no one on Kaua'i of sufficient rank to become the
ruling chief. The people turned to O'ahu where they found Kūali'i,
great-grandson of Ka-hā-malu-'ihi (no. 44), a chiefess with awesome *mana*.

	PARENTS		OFFSPRING
43. (1580 A.D.)	Kakuhihewa, k	Kaeaakalona, w	Kanekapuakakuhihewa, k
44. (1605 A.D.)	Kanekapuakakuhihewa, k	Kahamaluihi, w	Kahoowahakalani, k
45. (1630 A.D.)	Kahoowahakalani, k	Kawelolauhuki, w	Kauakahiakahoowaha, k
46. (1655 A.D.)	Kauakahiakahoowaha, k	Mahulua, w	Kualii, k
47. (1680 A.D.)	Kualii, k	Kalanikahimakeialii, w	Peleioholani, k
48. (1705 A.D.)	Peleioholani, k	[unknown]	Kaapuwai, w
49. (1730 A.D.)	Kaapuwai, w	Kaumeheiwa, k	Kamakahelei, w
50. (1755 A.D.)	Kamakahelei, w	Kiha, k	Keawe, k
			Lelemahalani, w
			Kaluaipihana, w
		Kanene, k	Kapuaamoku, w
		Kaeokulani, k	Kaumualii, k
51. (1780 A.D.)	Kaumualii, k	[unknown]	Humehume, k
		Kapuaamoku, w, pi'o	Keliiahonui, k
			Kekaulikekiniiki, w
		Naluahi, w	Kukiiahu, w
		Kawahinemakua, w	Nahinu, w
		Pakake, w	Keheakane, k

[k indicates *kane* (male) and w indicates *wahine* (female).]

SOURCES

Chapter 1
Kinohi Loa, *The Beginning*

Papa and Wākea
Beckwith, "Papa and Wakea," *Hawaiian Mythology,* pp. 293–306
———, "Kepelino's Traditions of Hawaii, Translated," Bernice Pauahi
   Bishop Museum, Bulletin 95
Fornander, "Story of the Islands' Formation and Origin of Race,"
   Collection, IV:2–31
———, "Legend of Hawaii-loa," *Collections,* VI:279–280
Fornander, *Polynesian Race,* I:112
Kepelino, *Tales and Traditions of Hawaii,* pp. 62–66, 190–192
Malo, *Hawaiian Antiquities,* pp. 3–5, 15–16, 28, 52, 69, 82, 85, 162,
   238–244
Pogue, *Moolelo of Ancient Hawaii,* pp. 43–44. See also the citations in
   Note 3.
Pukui/Elbert, *Hawaiian Dictionary,* p. 384

Ancient Kauaʻi Culture
Buck, Peter H., *Arts and Crafts of Hawaii,* pp. 12, 27, 30–31, 71, 77, 82,
   96, 102, 218, 272, 344, 424, 427, 433, 486, 514, 516, 517, 524–527,
   531, 542, 544, 551, 559, 560, 570, 571

Kū'alu-nui-paukū-mokumoku

Akina, *Menehune People* (typewritten manuscript in private collection)
Bennett, Wendell Clark, *Archeology of Kauai*. Site 16, p. 103
Gay, Francis, *Place Names of Kauai*
Lahainaluna Students Paper No. 15
Rice, *Hawaiian Legends*, p. 34
Wichman, "Ka Mo'olelo o Kahāpula," *Polihale*, pp. 41–52

Menehune

Akina, *Menehune People*
Bennett, *Archeology of Kauai*, Site 26, pp. 105–107. Site 39, p. 111.
    Site 109, p. 128
Dickey, Lyle, *The Stories of Wailua, Kauai*
Fornander, *Polynesian Race*, I: 55, 98–99, and II: 6, 23, 132
Hofgaard, Christopher B., *The Menehune Family*
Kaiwi, J. H., "Story of the Race of Menehunes of Kauai," *More Hawaiian
    Folktales*
Kawailiula, S. K., *A Short Story*
Kelsey, Theodore, *Notes*
Knudsen, A. F., "The Ditch the Menehunes Built," *Teller of Hawaiian
    Tales*, pp. 97–101
————, "The Ale Koko Fishpond," *Teller of Hawaiian Tales*, pp. 248–251
Lahainaluna Student Papers No. 15
Lahainaluna Student Papers No. 19
Luomala, Katherine, *The Menehune of Polynesia*
————, "Menehune, the Little People," *Voices on the Wind*, pp. 123–138
Rice, "The Menehune," *Hawaiian Legends*, pp. 33–46
Thrum, "Story of the Race of Menehunes," *More Hawaiian Folktales*,
    pp. 214–219
————, "The Legend of Kanehunamoku," *Hawaiian Annual 1916*
Wichman, "Manini-holo," *Kauai Tales*, pp. 149–155
————"'Alekoko," *More Kaua'i Tales*, pp. 27–32

Concerning the Menehune. There are those who argue that the Menehune
never existed, that they were figments of imagination, similar to the Irish
leprechaun or Norwegian brownie. This view was first offered by Christopher B. Hofgaard, *The Menehune Family.* This view was strengthened
by Katherine Luomala, *The Menehune of Polynesia and Other Mythical Little
People of Oceania.* Both were Scandinavian and undoubtedly heard stories
of their native brownies and other little mischievous people who haunt the
Scandinavian forests.

    N. B. Emerson, according to a note in Theodore Kelsey's folder in the
Hawai'i State Archives, defines "Menehune" as stone laborers, saying that
mene is the blunt edge of an adz and *hune* is a poor man, destitute of property.

He goes on to say: "In general the Menehune people were skilled craftsmen who worked for their living—the maka'āinana—but their adventures and exploits were veiled in mystery largely because of the way their deeds were related by storytellers. That they worked only under cover of night and finished their assigned tasks before daylight, could easily be explained when it is known that Hawaians generally in their methods of cooperative living known as Lima-lau and Paulima, allowed only one day to finish an assigned task. They never left their project to be finished at another time. The Hawaiians designated a twenty-four-hour period, which we call *day*, by the term *pō* (which we construe as night). Ho'okāhipō is the time between the rising of one moon and the rising of the one following."

Ola

Akina, *Menehune People*

Beckwith, *Hawaiian Mythology*, pp. 329, 444

Bennett, *Archaeology of Kauai*, Sites 19, 20, 21, p. 104

Fornander, "Story of Hanaaumoe," *Collection*, IV:476–483

Gay, *Place Names of Kauai*

Ii, John Papa, *Fragments of Hawaiian History*, pp. 33, 35–45

Kamakau, *Ruling Chiefs of Hawaii*, pp. 337, 399.

Knudsen, A. F., "Story of King Ola," in Thrum, *More Hawaiian Folklore*, pp. 94–97

Neal, Marie, *In Hawaiian Gardens*, pp. 97–99 for details of the *loulu* palm itself.

Pukui/Elbert, *Hawaiian Dictionary*, various entries

Rice, "The Destruction of the Akua on Niihau," *Hawaiian Legends*, p. 68

Thrum, *Hawaiian Almanac and Annual 1907*, pp. 40, 53–64.

———, "The Legend of Kanehunamoku; The Phantom Isle, Home of the Menehunes and Mus," *Hawaiian Annual 1916*

———, "Story of the Race of Menehunes," *More Hawaiian Folktales*, pp. 214–219

Wichman, "Kiki-a-Ola," *Polihale*, pp. 53–64.

Kāne-a-Lohi

Akina, *Menehune People*

Gay, Charles, *Notes*

Gay, Roland L., "A Warning of Danger Ahead," *Hawaii Tales of Yesteryear*

Rice, "The Bird Man," *Hawaiian Legends*, pp. 47–48

Wichman, "Lauhaka," *Kauai Tales*, pp. 119–122.

Mū-'ai-mai'a

Anonymous, *Mū o Laau-haele-mai*

Bennett, *Archaeology of Kauai*, Site 11, p. 152

Knudsen, *Teller of Tales*, pp. 39–44
Lydgate, Rev. J. M., "The Winning of the Mu-ai-Maia Maiden,"
pp. 25–27
———, "The Affairs of the Wainiha Hui," *Hawaiian Almanac and
Annual, 1913*, pp. 125–137

Ka-iki-pa'a-nānea
Fornander, "Legend of Kepakailiula," *Collections*, IV:498–515.
Wichman, "Ka-iki-pa'a-nānea," *Polihale*, pp. 65–76.

Chapter 2
Nā Holokai, *The Seafarers*

Nana'ulu and 'Ulu
Beckwith, *Hawaiian Mythology*, pp. 49, 293, 298, 356, 376, 394–395
Fornander, *Polynesian Race*, I:166–168, 188, 189, 190–207, 249; II:5, 6, 12,
13, 21, 22, 23–25, 27, 28, 31, 38, 39, 44, 45–47, 48, 50, 57, 70, 74, 79
Johnson, *Kumulipo*, pp. 48, 63, 74, 81, 82, 84, 91, 112, 122–124, 158
Kamakau, *Tales and Traditions*, pp. 36, 42, 76, 97, 108, 135
Westervelt, "Sons of Kii," *Hawaiian Historical Legends*, pp. 47–64

Puna-nui-ka-ia-'āina
Akina, *Menehune People*
Fornander, *Polynesian Race*, II:45–46
Rice, "The Menehune," *Hawaiian Legends*, pp. 33–46

Puna-'ai-koā-i'i
Fornander, *Polynesian Race*, I:166, 206, II:45–46, 53–54
Kalakaua, "The Triple Marriage of Laa-mai-kahiki," *Legends and Myths of
Hawaii*, pp. 124–125
Kamakau, *Tales and Traditions*, p. 106, where his name is spelled Puna-'ai-
koa'e

Mo'ikeha
Beckwith, "The Moikeha–La'a Migration," *Hawaiian Mythology*,
pp. 352–362
Cartwright, Bruce, *Some Aliis of the Migratory Period*
Fornander, *Collections*, IV:20
———, "Kaao no Kaulanapokii," *Collection*, IV:560–569
———, "History of Moikeha," *Collection*, IV:112–159, 163, 169
———, "Kaulanapokii," *Collection*, IV:560–568
———, *Polynesian Race*, I:189, 97–199, 202, 204, 206, 249
———, *Polynesian Race*, II:6, 9, 11, 19, 31, 40, 43, 45, 47, 48, 49–56, 60,
62, 65, 70, 88, 92, 93, 134

Henry, "Mo'ikeha," *Voyaging Chiefs*, 133–152
Kahoewa'a, *The Legend of Keanini'ulaokalani*
Kalakaua, "The Triple Marriage of Laa-mai-kahiki," *Legends and Myths of Hawaii*, pp. 115–135
Kamakau, *Tales and Traditions*, pp. 36, 77, 85, 86, 103–106, note 12, p. 121
Knudsen, "The Lost Princess," *Teller of Hawaiian Tales*, pp. 140–143
Lahainaluna Students Papers No. 19
Malo, *Hawaiian Antiquities*, Ch. 4, pp. 5–9
Pukui, *'Olelo No'eau*, No. 467
Pukui/Elbert, *Hawaiian Dictionary*
Thrum, "Keanini-ulao-ka-lani," *More Hawaiian Folktales*, pp. 220–227
Westervelt, "Ke-au-nini," *Hawaiian Legends of Ghosts and Ghost-gods*

La'a-mai-Kahiki

Andrews, *A Dictionary of the Hawaiian Language*, entry for *ka-na-wai*
Fornander, *Collection*, VI:430, 444
———, *Polynesian Race*, I:204, II: 56, 62
Henry, *Ancient Tahiti*, p. 357
Kamakau, *People of Old*, pp. 7, 11–17, 59
Malo, *Hawaiian Antiquities*, p. 7, p. 151, note 25, pp. 159–160
Pukui/Elbert, *Hawaiian Dictionary*, 1957 edition, entries for Lono-i-ka-'ou-ali'i and La'a-mai-kahiki and *kānāwai*

Kila

Fornander, "Legend of Kila," *Collection*, IV:160–173
———, *Polynesian Race*, II:54–56

Ka-'ili-lau-o-ke-koa

Andrews, Robert Standard, *A Legend of Kauai*
Dickey, *Stories of Wailua, Kauai*
Emerson, *Unwritten Literature of Hawaii*, pp. 135–137
Haleole, *The Hawaiian Romance of Laieikawai*
Rice, *Hawaiian Legends*, pp. 106–108
Thrum, *More Hawaiian Folk Tales*, pp. 123–135
Wichman, "Ka Paio o 'Ōpaeka'a," *Polihale*, pp. 139–148

Concerning place names. In the chant that begins *"E pi'i i ka nahele,"* the chanter refers to certain places and people perhaps unfamiliar to modern readers. Here, then, is a list of these references.

Ka-wai-kini. The highest peak on Kaua'i. From its summit the entire Wailua river area can be seen.

Pihana-ka-lani. One of the sacred places of worship along the Wailua river; its exact location has been lost.

Ka-hale-lehua. Goddess of the rain and sister of Ka-ua-kahi-aliʻi.

Ka-ua-kahi-aliʻi. Foster son of Waha, the sorceress; brother of Ka-hale-lehua.

Ka-ʻili-lau-o-ke-koa. Beautiful grandchild of Moʻikeha and Hina-ʻa-ulu-ā. She was a champion surfer.

Hoʻoipo-i-ka-malanai. Sobriquet of Hina-ʻa-ulu-ā, wife of Moʻikeha; grandmother of Ka-ʻili-lau-o-ke-koa.

Lehua-wehe. Blossoms that had fallen from a *lehua* tree at the junction of the north and south forks of the Wailua river floated one after another downriver until they reached the sea. Here, on the south side near the rocks, they gathered in an eddy named Lehua-wehe. The spot was a well-known surfing area. Lehua-wehe was also the *kahu* (guardian) of Ka-ʻili-lau-o-ke-koa and a sister of Ka-ua-kahi-aliʻi.

Wai-ehu. The waterfall in the south branch of the Wailua river.

Kewā. A wetlands in Kapaʻa where reed grass grew. It was a favorite spot for lovers, since the grass was not only soft to lie upon but tall enough to hide them.

Maka-iwa. Another famous surfing area at Wailua, the favorite of Ka-ʻili-lau-o-ke-koa.

Wailua-nui-hōano. The lower portion of the Wailua river where, from the time of Hina-ʻa-ulu-ā's great-grandfather, the Puna ruling chiefs had their principal domicile.

ʻAliō. The beach at Wailua, bound on one side by Hikina-a-ka-lā and on the other by Kukui, both places of worship.

Chapter 3
Wā Pōpilikia, *Troubled Times*

Kānāwai

Fornander, *Collection*, VI:402

Johnson, *Kumulipo*, 59

Kamakau, *People of Old*, pp. 11–18

Pukui / Elbert, *Hawaiian Dictionary*, entries for *pule oʻo, puʻua, maea*

ʻAhukini-a-Laʻa

Dickey, *The Stories of Wailua*

Fornander, *Polynesian Race*, I:92

Kamakau, *Tales and Traditions*, p. 136

Luomala, *Maui-of-a-thousand-tricks*

Malo, *Hawaiian Antiquities*, ch. 46

Pukui / Elbert, *Hawaiian Dictionary*, entry for *puʻua*

Westervelt, *Legends of Maui*
Wichman, "Ka Manuahi," *Polihale*

Kama-hano

Akina, *Ike Hou I Ku Lulu-o-Moikeha*
Dickey, *Legends of Wailua*
Fornander, *Collection*, V:372–375
Pukui / Elbert, *Hawaiian Dictionary*, entry for *maea*
Westervelt, *Legends of Old Honolulu*

Lu'anu'u

Akina, "Seeing Lulu-o-Moikeha on the Plain of Kapa'a Once More"
Beckwith, *Hawaiian Mythology*, pp. 414–415
Dickey, *Legends of Wailua*
Fornander, *Collection*, V:136–140, 372–373
———, *Polynesian Race*, II:92
Kamakau, *Tales and Traditions*, pp. 101, 147
Wichman, "Palila," "Kia-kaka o Pā'ā," and "Ka Ulu Maia a Palila,"
    Polihale

Concerning Lu'anu'u. Note that Kamakau says that Lu'anu'u's father was Laka
and his mother Hīkāawelena, a chiefess of the Pa'ahoa rains of Waimea,
Kaua'i.

Lu'anu'u's name recalls an ancestor of his, born eleven generations after
the world flood from which Nu'u and his family escaped destruction. This
was Lu'anu'u (*Second Nu'u*), the ancestor from whom two groups of Kaua'i
residents were descended. Lu'anu'u, with his chiefly wife, Me'e-hiwa, had
Ka-lani-menehune, considered the ancestor of the Menehune people, the
extraordinary engineers of Kaua'i. Ka-lani-menehune had twin sons, Aholoholo and Kinilau. Aholoholo was renowned for his swiftness.

With his wife Ahu, Lu'anu'u had Kū-nāwao, and from him descended the
people called Ka Poe Mū-'ai-mai'a (*Banana-eating People*). Kū-nāwao had
several younger brothers and became a wanderer.

Kūkona

Bennett, Site 22, *Archeology of Kauai*
Fornander, "A Lamentation for Keawekalohe," *Collection*, VI:426
———, *Collection*, V:314–363
———, *Polynesian Race*, pp. 67–69
Kalakaua, "The Iron Knife," *Legends and Myths of Hawaii*, pp. 175–205
Malo, "Ch. 48, Concerning Kamaluohua," *Hawaiian Traditions*
Rice, *Hawaiian Legends*, pp. 51–53
Westervelt, *Legends of Old Honolulu*, pp. 246–277

Chapter 4
Wā Maika'i, Good Times

Introduction

Anonymous, *Life in Early Hawai'i, The Ahupua'a*
Fornander, *Polynesian Race,* I:249
Gutmanis, June, *Na Pule Kahiko: Ancient Hawaiian Prayers*
Kamakau, *Tales and Traditions*
Malo, *Hawaiian Antiquities*
Pogue, John F., *Moolelo of Ancient Hawaii*
Pukui/Elbert, *Hawaiian Dictionary,* entries for *kīloulou* and *uhiuhi*

Contemporary Rulers

	Kaua'i	O'ahu	Maui	Hawai'i
1480 A.D.	Kahakuokāne	Kalonaiki	Kahekili I	Kiha
1505 A.D.	Kūwalupaukūmoku	Piliwale	Kawaokaohele	Liloa
1530 A.D.	Kahakumakapaweo	Kukaniloko	Piilani	Umi-a-Liloa
1555 A.D.	Kalanikukuma	Kalaimanuia	Kihapiilani	Keawe-nui-a-Umi
1580 A.D.	Kahakumakalina	Kaihikapu-a-Manuia	Kamalālāwalu	Lono-i-ka-makahiki
1605 A.D.	Kamakapu	Kakuhihewa	Kauhi-a-kama	

Mano-ka-lani-pō

Dickey, *Stories of Wailua, Kauai*
———, *String Figures from Hawaii,* p. 132
Emerson, *Pele and Hiiaka*
———, *Unwritten Literature,* pp. 40, 228
Fornander, *Collection,* V:314 ffp., 343, 492–498; VI:428, 457–459, 516
———, "A Lamentation for Keawekalohe," *Collections,* VI:426
———, *Polynesian Race,* I:184, 187, 195–196; II:65, 73, 88, 136, 169, 231, 278–288, 291, 293, 295–297, 371–399
Iarafrie, Tone Iahuanu Tahuria, "A Hawaiian Legend of a Terrible War Between Pele-of-the-eternal-fires and Waka-of-the-shadowy-waters"
Kamakau, *Tales and Traditions,* p. 11
Mu-o-Laau-haele-mai
Rice, *Hawaiian Legends,* pp. 7–17
Westervelt, *Legends of Old Honolulu, Hawaii,* pp. 258–266
Wichman, *Pele Ma*

Kaumaka-a-Mano

Beckwith, *Hawaiian Mythology,* pp. 49–52
Dickey, *String Figures from Hawaii,* p. 82

Fornander, *Polynesian Race*, pp. 93–94
Johnson, *Kumulipo*, pp. 58, 118, 139
Kamakau, *Ka Poʻe Kahiko*, p. 11
Kelsey, *Place Names of Kauai*
Kepelino, *Traditions of Hawaii*, p. 12
Malo, *Hawaiian Antiquities*, pp. 150–151, 152, 155, 157, 167, 174
Pukui/Elbert, *Hawaiian Dictionary*, entries for *puʻukoāliʻi, Ka-hō-āliʻi,* and
 niuhi.
Rice, "The small wise boy and the little fool," *Hawaiian Legends*,
 pp. 49–50
Thrum, *Hawaiian Almanac*, 1907, p. 42
———, *Hawaiian Almanac*, 1910, pp. 59–60
Wichman, "Nā Kia Manu a me Nā Moa Makanahele," *More Kauai Tales*,
 pp. 113–118.
———, "Nā Kia Manu a me Nā Maiʻa," *More Kauai Tales*, pp. 125–132

Ka-haku-a-Kāne

Fornander, *Polynesian Race*, I:195, 249, II:71, 93–94, 205
Johnson, *Kumulipo*, pp. 58, 135–136, 138

Concerning Ka-haku-a-Kāne. Ka-ulu-lā'au, first cousin of Ka-haku-a-Kāne's
Maui wife Kapō-naenae, was very mischievous as a youngster, and his father
eventually banished him to the island of Lānaʻi. That island was overridden
with ghosts and goblins who rendered Lānaʻi uninhabitable. Ka-ulu-lā'au
outwitted all the evil spirits and rendered Lānaʻi a fit place to live once
again. Undoubtedly, the story of Ka-ulu-lā'au was told at the court of
Ka-haku-a-Kāne.

Kū-walu-paukū-moku

Fornander, *Race*, I: 195, 249, II:94
Kamakau, *Tales and Traditions*, p. 11
Johnson, *Kumulipo*, pp. 54, 135, 138
Neal, *Hawaiian Gardens*, p. 500
Pukui/Elbert, *Hawaiian Dictionary*, entries for *hame* and *pīkele*
Westervelt, "The Ghost of Wahaula Temple," *Ghosts and Ghost-gods*

Ka-haku-maka-paweo

Fornander, *Collection*, VI: 422–424
Fornander: *Polynesian Race*, I: 195, 249, II:91, 94, 131, 291, 292
Johnson, *Kumulipo*, p. 135
Kamakau: *Ka Poʻe Kahiko*, p. 11

Ka-lani-kukuma

Fornander: *Collections*, V:72–135
Fornander: *Polynesian Race*, II:112, 292

Johnson, *Kumulipo*, p. 135
Kamakau, *Ruling Chiefs*, pp. 36–41
Nakuina, Moses K., *Laomaomao, Calabash of Winds*
Pukui, Mary Kawena, Samuel H. Elbert and Esther T. Mookini,
    Place Names of Hawaii
Pukui/Elbert, *Hawaiian Dictionary*, entries for *Hikauhi* and *pai'ea*
Rice, *Hawaiian Legends*, pp. 69–89
Thrum, *More Hawaiian Folktales*, pp. 53–67
Westervelt, "Pikoi the Rat-killer," *Legends of Old Honolulu*, pp. 157–172

Concerning Kamili. 'Ili-hiwa-lani's wife Kamili belonged to the chiefly line of the 'Ewa district of O'ahu. She was descended from Maweke and thus joined one genealogical line to another. Her grandfather was Haka who lived in Lihu'e in the 'Ewa district of O'ahu. "He was a stingy, rapacious, and ill-natured chief, who paid no regard to either his chiefs or his commoners. As a consequence they revolted from him, made war upon him, and besieged him in his fortress, called Waewae, near Lihu'e. During one night of the siege, an officer of his guards, whom he had ill-treated, surrendered the fort to the rebel chiefs, who entered and killed Haka whose life was the only one spilt on the occasion." Kamili's sister Kaulala was an ancestress of Kūali'i, who became ruler of Kaua'i about 1700 A.D."

Concerning Pāka'a's education. These are the things Pāka'a learned: the natural history of the land, including the names of each and every *ahupua'a* on each island and what each could produce. He learned how to read the omens in the clouds. He could read the rainbow colors at the edges of the stars, the way they twinkled and the way they dimmed when a storm was coming. He learned how to tell when the sea would be calm and when there would be great swells that send billows crashing across the beaches. He learned how to paddle a canoe and how to right a canoe that was upset at sea. He learned all the arts of navigation, the path of the stars, the directions of winds and ocean swells, the cloud formations, the flight of birds and the path of fish. He already had been taught the names of all the winds by his mother Lao-ma'oma'o, where they came from and what they could do. He learned how to care for his chief, which foods he liked to eat after his cup of 'awa, how he liked his clothing scented, and all the whims and caprices indulged in by the high chiefs of long ago.

Ka-haku-maka-lina

Fornander, "Story of Lonoikamakahiki, *Collection*, IV:256–363
———, "Legend of Kapakohana," *Collection*, V: 208–212
———, *Polynesian Race*, II: 104, 292
Johnson, *Kumulipo*, pp. 56, 59, 85, 135
Kamakau, *Ruling Chiefs*, pp. 51–52, 448
———, *Tales and Traditions*, p. 9

Maka, Jacob, *Personal communication, July 1949*. He told me Hoʻohila's
story as we stood inside her small cave watching the waves crash
against the cliff. This is also the site where the first beach *naupaka* was
created and the mountain *naupaka* appeared on the ridge above.
Pukui/Elbert, *Hawaiian Dictionary*, entry for *kai heheʻe*
Wichman, "Naupaka," *Polihale*, pp. 175–178

Concerning spelling. The last part of his name is either *lina* or *liua*. This confusion may arrive from misreading an original handwritten manuscript, for
handwriting in those days did not carefully distinguish between an "n" or
a "u." Kamakau, in his various newspaper articles, uses both *lina* and *liua*.
Fornander consistently uses *lina*, and so I prefer to continue this usage.

Kama-kapu
Fornander, *Polynesian Race*, II: 272–275, 292
Johnson, *Kumulipo*, pp. 52–60, 69
Kamakau, *People of Old*, pp. 9, 22
———, *Tales and Traditions*, pp. 87, 88
McKinzie, *Hawaiian Genealogies*, I:15, 31, 80

Chapter 5
Kaua, War

The Kawelo Family
Dickey, *The Stories of Wailua, Kauaʻi*
Fornander, "A Lamentation for Kalaiulumoku," *Collection*, VI: 423, lines
30–37
———, "Legend of Kawelo," *Collection*, V:2–71
———, "A Story of Kawelo" by D. Kamakea, *Collection*, V:694–772
———, *Polynesian Race*, II:292, 293
Fox, *The Threshold of the Pacific*, pp. 162–169
Green, *The Legend of Kawelo*
Henry, *Ancient Tahiti*, pp. 304–305
Ka Moolelo hiwahiwa o Kawelo
Lahainaluna Student Paper No. 19
Remy, "The Story and Song of Kawelo," *Contributions of a Venerable
Native*
Rice, *Hawaiian Legends*, pp. 54–67
Thrum, *Maulili*, Hawaiian Almanac and Annual for 1907
———, Hawaiian Almanac and Annual for 1911, 9.119–128
———, *Heiau of Hawaii*
Westervelt, "The Legends of Kawelo," *More Hawaiian Folktales*,
pp. 149–163
———, "Kawelo," *Hawaiian Legends of Old Honolulu*, pp. 173–188

Chapter 6
Moku, *The End*

Kūali'i
Fornander, *Collection*, IV:370–395.
————, *Collection*, V:28–29
————, *Polynesian Race*, II:272–288

Pele-i'ō-hōlani
Fornander, *Polynesian Race*, II:282–284, 290, 295–297
Kalākaua, "The Cannibals of Halemanu," *The Legends and Myths of Hawai'i*, p. 371
Kamakau, *Ruling Chiefs*, pp. 92–97, 130, 194
————, *Tales and Traditions*, p. 117
Stokes, *New Bases for Hawaiian Chronology*, p. 41

Concerning Kāne-'ai'ai. The canoe *Kāne'ai'ai* was finally abandoned on a Kaua'i beach where it slowly rotted. It was a double canoe with a platform between the hulls. Each hull was built up with planks sewn together with coconut husk cords. It could hold between 120 and 160 men with all the food, water, and armament needed. Its name may perhaps be translated as *Man who lives on the resources of others*, for certainly only ruling chiefs could command such resources as it took to manufacture, provision, and man such a craft.

Concerning Ka-lani-'ōpu'u. Pele-i'ō-hōlani is the reputed father of Ka-lani-'ōpu'u who was the paramount Hawai'i island chief at the time of Captain Cook's arrival. Ka-lani-'ōpu'u's mother was Ka-maka'i-moku who had come to Waikele, O'ahu, to visit her mother and brothers. Here she met and lived with Pele-i'ō-hōlani. He gave her a *lei 'opu'u*, a neck ornament made of a whale tooth shaped into a flower bud. This had once belonged to Kūali'i. Then Ka-lani-nui-a-mamao, a high chief of Hawai'i, took her as his wife, even though she was pregnant. When her son was born, Ka-maka'i-moku named him Ka-lei-'ōpu'u, but others always called him Ka-lani-'ōpu'u.
At the time of the meeting of Alapa'i-nui and Pele-i'ō-hōlani, Ka-maka'i-moku had become the wife of Alapa'i-nui.

Concerning Kapupu'u. The official English version, written many years later by James King from Cook's logs, said that the first Hawaiian killed had been one of a crowd menacing the crew of a long boat seeking to replenish the ship's water supply. However, it seems to me that if the crowd had really been menacing, killing one of them would have resulted immediately in battles. Yet the following day Cook landed and walked about the village unmolested and unaccompanied except by Weber, who was busy drawing the scenes before him, and perhaps one other man. Only the fact that Ka-pupuʻu had openly defied his chief, and the prevailing concept that if a thief was caught, it was his fault and his assassin was never blamed, kept Cook alive.

Ka-maka-helei

Bennett, *Archeology of Kauai,* Site 137
Desha, *Kamehameha and his Warrior Kekūkahupiʻo,* pp. 430–431
Ii, *Fragments,* pp. 79–83
Kamakau, *Ruling Chiefs,* pp. 68–69,162, 169
Lahainaluna Students Paper No. 15
Lahainaluna Student Papers No. 19
Wells, *An Authentic Narrative of a Voyage,* I:134

Concerning Lele-mahoe-lani. It is possible that Weber's portrait of a Hawaiian chiefess is that of Lele-mahoe-lani. Later on, it was whispered that Ka-umu-aliʻi himself was born from this affair between his older sister and the English captain since Ka-umu-aliʻi is always described as being shorter than most aliʻi, with paler skin and a Roman nose (all considered *haole* attributes). Ka-umu-aliʻi was born two years later in 1780 and there is no doubt that his mother was Ka-maka-helei and his father Ka-ʻeo-kū-lani.

Ka-umu-aliʻi

Bingham, *A Residence of Twenty-one Years in the Sandwich Islands,* p. 292
Desha, *Kamehameha,* pp. 429–442.
Fornander, *Collection,* III:246, n. 7.
Ii, *Fragments,* pp. 79–83.
Kamakau, *Ruling Chiefs,* pp. 195–196, 252–253, 255–265, 318
Kuykendall, *The Hawaiian Kingdom,* pp. 49–51, 56–59, 61, 74–76, 88, 96, 434
Stokes, *New Bases,* p. 46.

Concerning Ka-umu-aliʻi's Sailors. Rowbottom and John Williams, along with Coleman, had been left on Niihau on October 27, 1791 by Captain John Kendrick of the *Lady Washington* with the orders to collect sandalwood and pearls. A year earlier Captain William Douglas of the *Grace* had left two men on Kauaʻi to collect sandalwood. Their captains did not return as promised and all five men were taken in by Ka-umu-aliʻi. Williams was still alive at the time of the Mahele and made a claim for land.

The Revolution of 1824

Bingham, *A Residence of Twenty-One Years in the Sandwich Islands*
Emerson, *Unwritten Literature,* pp. 255–256
Kamakau, *Ruling Chiefs,* p. 269
Stewart, *A Residence in the Sandwich Islands,* pp. 313–315, 319–320

BIBLIOGRAPHY

Akina, Joseph A. *"Seeing Lulu-o-Moikeha on the Plain of Kapaʻa Once More."* *Nupepa Kuokoa*, May 2, 1913. Translation by Mary K. Pukui. Bernice P. Bishop Museum Library.

———. *"The Story of the Menehune People."* Unpublished holographic manuscript in Hawaiian, transcribed by Frances Frazier, 1904. (In private collection.)

Andrews, Lorrin. *A Dictionary of the Hawaiian Language*. Rutland, VT: Charles E. Tuttle Company, 1974 reprint.

Andrews, Robert Standard. A Legend of Kauai. *Par. Pac.*, 24 (Feb., Mar., Apr., and May 1911). From the Hawaiian of A. H. Ahakuelo, written in 1901.

Aukai, S. *"The Legend of Kealohiwai."* Typewritten manuscript. (In private collection.)

Barrère, Dorothy B., Mary Kawena Pukui, and Marion Kelly. *Hula: Historical Perspectives*. Pacific Anthropological Records No. 30, Department of Anthropology, Bernice P. Bishop Museum. Honolulu: Bishop Museum Press, 1980.

Beckwith, Martha Warren. *Hawaiian Mythology*. Honolulu: University of Hawaiʻi Press, 1970.

———. "Kepelino's Traditions of Hawaii, Translated" (text *ca.* 1860), Bernice Pauahi Bishop Museum, Bulletin 95, Honolulu: Bishop Museum Press, 1932.

Beniamina, Jean Ilei. Personal communication.

148

Bennett, Wendell Clark. *Archeology of Kauai*. Bernice P. Bishop Museum Bulletin No. 80. Millwood, NY: Kraus, 1976 reprint.

Bingham, Hiram. *A Residence of Twenty-One Years in the Sandwich Islands*. Hartford: Hezekiah Huntington, 1849.

Buck, Peter H. *Vikings of the Sunrise*. New York: Frederick A. Stokes Company, 1938.

Cartright, Bruce. *Some Aliis of the Migratory Period*. Bernice P. Bishop Museum Occasional Papers, Volume X, Number 7. Honolulu: Bishop Museum Press, 1933.

Ching, Francis K. W., Stephen L. Palama, and Catherine Stauder. *The Archaeology of Kona, Kauaʻi: Na Ahupuaʻa Weliweli, Paʻa, Māhāʻulepū*. Hawaiian Archaeological Journal, 1974.

Clark, John R. K. *The Beaches of Kauai*. Honolulu: University of Hawaiʻi Press, 1989.

A Collection of Voyages and Travels from the Discovery of America to the Commencement of the Nineteenth Century. 28 vols. London: Printed for Richard Phillips, Bridge Street, Blackfriars; by J. Gold, Shoe-land, 1809.

Damon, Ethel M. *Koamalu: A Story of Pioneers on Kauai and of What They Built in That Island Garden*. Honolulu: Privately printed, 1931.

Desha, Stephen L. *Kamehameha and his Warrior Kekūhaupiʻo*. Translated by Frances N. Frazier. Honolulu: Kamehameha Schools Press, 2000.

Dickey, Lyle A. *Hanalei Place Names*. Kauai Historical Society Paper No. 105, 1934.

———. "The Portrait of Queen Hina." Carbon of typewritten manuscript, April 29, 1929. (In private collection.)

———. *String Figures from Hawaii including Some from New Hebrides and Gilbert Islands*. Bernice P. Bishop Museum Bulletin 54. Millwood: Kraus, 1985 reprint.

———. *The Stories of Wailua, Kauai*. Kauai Historical Society Paper No. 110, 1915.

Dole, C. S. "National Park for Garden Island." *Paradise of the Pacific*, December 1916.

Earle, Timothy. *Economic and Social Organization of a Complex Chiefdom: The Halelea District, Kauaʻi, Hawaii*. Museum of Anthropology, University of Michigan, No. 63. Ann Arbor: University of Michigan Press, 1978.

Ellis, Harriet. "The Legend of Niumalu Fishpond." Hawaiian Legends Submitted by the Pupils of the Kamehameha School for Girls for the Martha Beckwith Prize, 1942.

Ellis, William. *A Narrative of a Tour through Hawaii*. Advertiser Series no. 2. Honolulu: Hawaiian Gazette.

Emerson, Nathaniel B. *Pele and Hiiaka*. Rutland, VT: Charles E. Tuttle Company, 1978 reprint.

———. *Unwritten Literature of Hawaii: The Sacred Songs of the Hula*. Rutland, VT: Charles E. Tuttle Company, 1965 reprint.

Emory, Kenneth P. "The Ruins of Kee, Haena." Typewritten manuscript. In private collection.

Ferreira, Juliette L., "Lahemanu." Hawaiian Legends Submitted by the Pupils of the Kamehameha School for Girls for the Martha Beckwith Prize, 1939.

———. "The Story of the Caterpillar." Hawaiian Legends Submitted by the Pupils of the Kamehameha School for Girls for the Martha Beckwith Prize, 1938.

Fornander, Abraham. *An Account of the Polynesian Race, Its Origins and Migrations, and the Ancient History of the Hawaiian People to the Times of Kamehameha I.* Rutland, VT: Charles E. Tuttle Company, 1969 reprint.

———. *Collection of Hawaiian Antiquities and Folk-lore.* Edited by Thomas G. Thrum. Bernice P. Bishop Museum Memoirs 4, 5, 6. Honolulu: Bernice P. Bishop Museum, 1916–1919.

Gay, Francis. *Place Names of Kauai.* Typewritten transcription, Bernice P. Bishop Museum Library.

Gilman, G. D. *Journal of a Canoe Voyage along the Kauai Palis, made in 1845.* Papers of the Hawaiian Historical Society No. 14. Honolulu: Paradise of the Pacific, 1908.

Goodale, Holbrook. Personal Communication.

Green, Laura C. *The Legend of Kawelo.* Edited by Martha Warren Beckwith. Poughkeepsie, NY: Vassar College, 1929.

Gutmanis, June. *Na Pule Kahiko, Ancient Hawaiian Prayers.* Honolulu: Editions Limited. 1983.

Hadley, Thelma H., and Margaret S. Williams. *Kauai, the Garden Island of Hawaii; and Guide Book.* Lihue, HI: Garden Island, 1962.

[Haleole] *The Hawaiian Romance of Laieikawai,* with introduction and translation by Martha Warren Beckwith, Reprint of the Thirty-third Annual Report of the Bureau of American Ethnology. Washington, D.C.: Government Printing Office, 1918.

Handy, E. S. Craighill. *The Hawaiian Planter,* volume I. Bernice P. Bishop Museum Bulletin 161. Millwood: Kraus, 1985 reprint.

Handy, E. S. Craighill, and Elizabeth Green Handy. *Native Planters in Old Hawaii; Their Life, Lore, and Environment.* Bernice P. Bishop Museum Bulletin 233. Honolulu: Bishop Museum Press, 1972.

Hanner, Ruth Knudsen. Personal communication.

Hashimoto, Jack. Personal communication.

Hashimoto, Thomas. Personal communication.

Henry, Teuria. *Ancient Tahiti.* Bernice P. Bishop Museum Bulletin 48. Millwood: Kraus, 1985 reprint.

Henry, Teuira, and others. *Voyaging Chiefs of Hawaii.* Honolulu: Noio, 1995.

"He Wahi Moolelo Hawaii." Translated by Mary K. Pukui. *Nupepa Kuakoa,* June 27, 1902. Bishop Museum Library.

Hinds, Norman E. A. *The Geology of Kauai and Niihau.* Bernice P. Bishop Museum Bulletin 71. Millwood, VT: Kraus, 1985 reprint.

Hiroa, Te Rangi (Peter H. Buck). *Arts and Crafts of Hawaii*. Bernice P. Bishop Museum Special Publication 45. Honolulu: Bishop Museum Press, 1957.

Hofgaard, C. B. "Who Were The Menehunes?" Honolulu: *Paradise of the Pacific*, May 1928.

Huddy, Charles. Personal communication.

I, Gabriel. Personal communication.

Iarafrie, Tone-Iahuanu-tahuria. *"A Hawaiian Legend of a Terrible War between Pele-of-the-eternal-fires and Waka-of-the-shadowy-waters."* Translated by Mary Pukui. *Ka Loea Kalaiaina*, May 13 to August 29, 1899. Bishop Museum Library.

Ii, John Papa. *Fragments of Hawaiian History*. Translated by Mary K. Pukui; edited by Dorothy B. Barrère. Honolulu: Bishop Museum Press, 1959.

[Ingraham, Captain Joseph.] *The Log of the Brig Hope called The Hope's Track among the Sandwich Islands, May 20, October 12, 1791*. Hawaiian Historical Society Reprints, No. 3. Honolulu: *Paradise of the Pacific*, 1918.

Irwin, Geoffrey. *The Prehistoric Exploration and Colonization of the Pacific*. Cambridge: Cambridge University Press, 1992.

Jarves, James J. *History of the Hawaiian or Sandwich Islands*. Boston: James Munroe and Company, 1843.

Joesting, Edward. *Kauai: A Separate Kingdom*. Honolulu: University of Hawai'i Press and Kauai Museum Association, 1984.

Johnson, Rubellite Kawena, *Kumulipo: Hawaiian Hymn of Creation*, Vol. I. Honolulu: Topgallant, 1981.

Judd, Henry P. *Hawaiian Proverbs and Riddles*. Bernice Pauahi Bishop Museum Bulletin 77. Honolulu: Bishop Museum Press, 1930.

Kalākaua, His Hawaiian Majesty King David. *The Legends and Myths of Hawaii*. Rutland, VT: Charles E. Tuttle Company, 1989 reprint.

Kamakau, Samuel Manaiakalani, *Ka Po'e Kahiko, The People of Old*. Translated from the newspaper *Ke Au 'Oko'a* by Mary Kawena Pukui, arranged and edited by Dorothy B. Barrère. Bernice P. Bishop Museum Special Publication 51. Honolulu: Bishop Museum Press, 1964.

———. *Nā Mo'olelo a ka Po'e Kahiko*. Honolulu: Bishop Museum Press, 1991.

———. *Ruling Chiefs of Hawaii*. Honolulu: The Kamehameha Schools Press, 1961.

———. *The Works of the People of Old. Nā Hana a ka Po'e Kahiko*. Honolulu: Bishop Museum Press, 1976.

Kame'eleihiwa, Lilikalā K. *A Legendary Tradition of Kamapua'a, the Hawaiian Pig-God*. Honolulu: Bishop Museum Press, 1996.

Kanoa, Charles K. "Nawailua," *Nupepe Kuokoa*, 1919.

Kaohe, Althea. Personal communication.

"The Kapahi Stone." *Makahonu Naumu*, May 22, 1940. Bishop Museum Library.

The Kauai Papers. Lihue, HI: Kauai Historical Society, 1991.

Kawailiula, S. K. "A Short Story." *Ka Hae Hawaii*, October 9, 1861. Bishop Museum Library.

Kekahuna, Henry P. *Kauai Place Names*. Kekahuna Collection, Archives of Hawaii, n.d.

———. *Miscellaneous Papers*. Kekahuna Collection, Archives of Hawaii, n.d.

———. *Notes*. Kekahuna Collection, Archives of Hawaii, n.d.

———. *The Story of Ualakaa*. Kekahuna Collection, Archives of Hawaii, n.d.

Kelsey, Theodore. *Hanalei District*. Kelsey Collection, Archives of Hawaii, n.d.

———. *Kauai Place Names*. Kelsey Collection, Archives of Hawaii, n.d.

———. *Place Names from Mr. Isaac Ka'iu*, Kelsey Collection, Archives of Hawaii, n.d.

———. *Place Names of Luahiwa of Kaua'i*. Kelsey Collection, Archives of Hawaii, n.d.

———. *Place Names of George Kalama of Papaaloa*. Kelsey Collection, Archives of Hawaii, n.d.

Kirch, Patrick Vinton. *Feathered Gods and Fishhooks: An Introduction to Hawaiian Archeology and Prehistory*. Honolulu: University of Hawai'i Press, 1985.

———. *The Lapita Peoples: Ancestors of the Oceanic World*. Cambridge, MA: Blackwell Publishers Inc., 1997.

———. *On the Road of the Winds: An Archaeological History of the Pacific Islands before European Contact*. Berkeley: University of California Press, 2000.

Knudsen, Eric A. *Queen Emma Goes to Alakai Swamp*. Kauai Historical Society Paper No. 67, 1940.

———. *Teller of Hawaiian Tales*. Honolulu: Coca-Cola Bottling Company, ca. 1945.

Kuykendall, Ralph S. *The Hawaiian Kingdom, 1778–1854: Foundation and Transformation*, Honolulu: University of Hawai'i, 1938.

Lahainaluna students. *Papers by Lahainaluna Students After Interviews with Old Residents of Kauai, 1885*. Bernice P. Bishop Museum Archives. Lahainaluna Students Papers. Hms. Misc. 43:

> No. 15. *Heiaus, Kauai, Fishing Grounds, Deep Fishing Grounds for letting down ropes, The Surfs of Waimea; Why This Surf Was Famous; Secret Caves of Waimea; The Heiaus of Waiawa; The Heiaus of Kekupua; Pools Belonging to Chiefs.*

> No. 16. *Information on ancient heiaus and famous stones of religious significance.*

> No. 18. *Fishing Grounds outside of the surf of Makaiwa as far as Wailua, Heiaus of and Kapaa, Well known things, Famous things mentioned by two men, Heiaus from Kapaa to Kealia.*

> No. 19. *Heiaus and Fishing grounds, Heiaus of Koloa, Fishing Grounds of Koloa, Record of a tour of Kauai (heiaus and fishing grounds), 1885, The heiaus of Nawiliwili, Sept. 16, 1885.*

Luomala, Katherine. *Maui-of-a-Thousand-Tricks; His Oceanic and European Biographers.* Bernice P. Bishop Museum Bulletin 198. Honolulu: Bishop Museum Press, 1949.

———. *The Menehune of Polynesia and Other Mythical Little People of Oceania.* Millwood, NY: Kraus, 1986 reprint

———. *Voices on the Wind.* Honolulu: Bishop Museum Press, 1955.

Lydgate, John M. "Charm and Romance of Haena, Kauai." Paradise of the Pacific, December 1922.

———. "Ka-umu-alii: The Last King of Kauai." *Hawaiian Historical Society,* 1915. Honolulu: Paradise of the Pacific, 1916.

Maka, Jacob. Personal communication.

Malo, David. *Hawaiian Antiquities,* Bernice P. Bishop Museum Special Publication 2, Second Edition. Translated by Dr. Nathaniel B. Emerson, 1898. Honolulu: Bishop Museum Press, 1951.

———. *Ka Mo'olelo Hawai'i, Hawaiian Traditions.* Translated by Malcolm Naea Chun. Honolulu: First People's Productions, 1987.

Mea Kakau. "He wahi moolelo Hawaii." *Nupepa Kuokoa,* June 27, 1902.

Meares, John. "Voyages Made in the Years 1788 and 1789 From China to the Northwest Coast of America, with an Introductory Narrative of a Voyage Performed in 1786, from Bengal, in the Ship 'Nootka.'" *Hawaiian Historical Society Reprint.*

Mills, Peter R. "A New View of Kaua'i as 'The Separate Kingdom' after 1810." *The Hawaiian Journal of History* 30, 1996.

Mookini, Esther "Kiki." Personal communication.

"Mu-o-Laau-haele-mai, The Mu of Laau-haele-mai, The People Who Were Called the Banana Eaters." Aloha Aina Puka La, October 24 to December 18, 1893.

"Na Iliili Hanau o Koloa." *Nupepe Kuokoa,* Feb. 10, 1911. Bishop Museum Library.

Nakuina, Moses K. *The Wind Gourd of La'amaomao.* Honolulu: Kalamakū Press, 1990.

"Na Makani o Kauai." *Ka Na'i Aupuni,* June 18–26, 1906. Translated by Mary Kawena Pukui. Collection of Francis Frazier.

Neal, Marie C. *In Gardens of Hawaii,* Bernice P. Bishop Museum Special Publication 50. Honolulu: Bishop Museum Press, 1965.

NeSmith, Keao. Personal communication.

Nordhoff, Charles. *Northern California, Oregon, and the Sandwich Islands.* New York: Harper & Bros., 1877.

Pogue, Reverend John F. *Moolelo of Ancient Hawaii.* Translated by Charles W. Kenn. Honolulu: Topgallant, 1978.

Portlock, Nathaniel. *A Voyage Round the World, Particularly to the North-west Coast of America: Performed in 1785, 1786, 1787 and 1788, in The King George and Queen Charlotte by Captains Portlock and Dixon.* London: Printed for John Stockdale, opposite Burlington House, Piccadilly; and George Goulding, James Street, Covent Garden, 1794.

Pukui, Mary Kawena. *Ancient Hulas of Kauai*. Kauai Historical Society Paper
No. 62, 1936.

———. *'Ōlelo No'eau: Hawaiian Proverbs and Poetical Sayings*. Bernice P.
Bishop Museum Special Publication No. 71. Honolulu: Bishop Museum
Press, 1983.

Pukui, Mary Kawena, and Samuel H. Elbert. *Hawaiian Dictionary* (Third
Edition). Honolulu: University of Hawai'i Press, 1986.

Pukui, Mary Kawena, Samuel H. Elbert, and Esther T. Mookini. *Place Names
of Hawaii*. Honolulu: University of Hawai'i Press, 1966.

Remy, M. Jules. *Contributions of a Venerable Native to the Ancient History of
the Hawaiian Islands*. Reno: Outbooks, 1979 reprint.

Rice, Charles A. Personal communication.

Rice, William Hyde. *Hawaiian Legends*. Bernice P. Bishop Museum Bulletin
No. 3. Honolulu: Bishop Museum Press, 1923.

Santos, Helena Maka. Personal communication.

Schmitt, Robert C. "The Population of Northern Kauai in 1847." In *Hawaii
Historical Review: Selected Readings*, edited by Richard A. Green. Honolulu: Hawaiian Historical Society, 1969.

Stillman, Charles K., compiler. *Hawaiian Place Names—Kauai*, unpublished
manuscript in the possession of Ruby Scott and Mary Luddington.

Stokes, John F. G. "The Hawaiian King." *Hawaiian Historical Society*, 1932.

———. "New Bases for Hawaiian Chronology." *Hawaiian Historical Society*,
1932.

Thrum, Thomas G. "Chronological Table of Important Events." *Hawaiian
Almanac and Annual for 1876*.

———. *Hawaiian Folktales*. Chicago: McClurg, 1907.

———. *More Hawaiian Folktales: A Collection of Native Legends and Traditions*. Chicago: McClurg, 1923.

———. "Who or What were the Menehunes?" *Hawaiian Almanac and
Annual, 1929*.

Tomonari-Tuggle, Myra Jean F. *An Archaeological Reconnaissance Survey: Na
Pali Coast State Park, Island of Kauai*. State of Hawaii., September 1989.

Vancouver, George. *A Voyage of Discovery to the North Pacific Ocean, and
Round the World, in the Years 1790, 1791, 1792, 1793, 1794 and 1795*.
Six vols. London. 1798.

Westervelt, William Drake. *Hawaiian Historical Legends*. New York: Fleming
H. Revell, 1923.

———. *Hawaiian Legends of Ghosts and Ghost-Gods*. Rutland, VT: Charles
E. Tuttle Company, 1963 reprint.

———. *Legends of Gods and Ghosts*. Boston: Geo. H. Ellis, Co., 1915.

———. *Legends of Old Honolulu, Hawaii*. Boston: Geo. H. Ellis Co., 1915.

———. Maui the Fisherman. *Paradise of the Pacific*, 75 (Mar. 1963), sou-
venir section, pp. xxii–xxiv.

Wichman, Frederick B. *Kauai Tales*. Honolulu: Bamboo Ridge Press, 1985.

————. *Polihale and other Kaua'i Legends*. Honolulu: Bamboo Ridge Press, 1991.

————. *More Kaua'i Tales*. Honolulu: Bamboo Ridge Press, 1997.

————. *Kaua'i, Ancient Place-Names and Their Stories*. Honolulu: University of Hawai'i Press, 1998.

————. *Pele Mā: Legends of Pele on Kaua'i*. Honolulu: Bamboo Ridge Press, 2001.

Wichman, Juliet Rice. Personal communication.

Wilkes, Charles. *Narrative of the United States Exploring Expedition during the years 1838, 1839, 1840, 1841, 1842*. Philadelphia: Lea and Blanchard, 1845.

INDEX

ABOUT THE AUTHOR

Frederick B. Wichman is the author of *Kauai Tales, Polihale, More Kauai Tales, Pele Mā,* and *Kauaʻi: Ancient Place-Names and Their Stories.* After teaching for many years, he returned to his home island of Kauaʻi and began to write. His stories have been adapted for theatre and hula performances, and in 1999 he was named a "Living Treasure" by the Kauaʻi Musuem.